CREATIVE PHYSICAL EDUCATION

Integrating Curriculum Through Innovative PE Projects

John Quay ▪ Jacqui Peters

HUMAN KINETICS

Library of Congress Cataloging-in-Publication Data

Quay, John, 1964-
 Creative physical education : integrating curriculum through innovative pe projects / John Quay
and Jacqui Peters.
      p. cm.
 Includes bibliographical references.
 ISBN 978-1-4504-2105-8 (soft cover) -- ISBN 1-4504-2105-9 (soft cover)
 1. Physical education and training--Curricula--United States. 2. Curriculum planning--United
States. I. Peters, Jacqui, 1967- II. Title.
 GV365.Q39 2012
 372.86'043--dc23

                                     2011045186

ISBN-10: 1-4504-2105-9 (print)
ISBN-13: 978-1-4504-2105-8 (print)

The web addresses cited in this text were current as of January 2012, unless otherwise noted.

Acquisitions Editor: Karalynn Thomson; **Developmental Editor:** Jacqueline Eaton Blakley; **Assistant Editor:** Anne Rumery; **Copyeditor:** Mary Rivers; **Permissions Manager:** Dalene Reeder; **Graphic Designer:** Bob Reuther; **Graphic Artist:** Dawn Sills; **Cover Designer:** Keith Blomberg; **CD Face Designer:** Susan Rothermel Allen; **Photographer (cover and interior):** Photos courtesy of John Quay and Jacqui Peters; **Art Manager:** Kelly Hendren; **Associate Art Manager:** Alan L. Wilborn; **Illustrations:** © Human Kinetics; **Printer:** United Graphics

Printed in the United States of America   10 9 8 7 6 5 4 3 2 1

The paper in this book is certified under a sustainable forestry program.

Human Kinetics
Website: www.HumanKinetics.com

United States: Human Kinetics
P.O. Box 5076
Champaign, IL 61825-5076
800-747-4457
e-mail: humank@hkusa.com

Canada: Human Kinetics
475 Devonshire Road Unit 100
Windsor, ON N8Y 2L5
800-465-7301 (in Canada only)
e-mail: info@hkcanada.com

Europe: Human Kinetics
107 Bradford Road
Stanningley
Leeds LS28 6AT, United Kingdom
+44 (0) 113 255 5665
e-mail: hk@hkeurope.com

Australia: Human Kinetics
57A Price Avenue
Lower Mitcham, South Australia 5062
08 8372 0999
e-mail: info@hkaustralia.com

New Zealand: Human Kinetics
P.O. Box 80
Torrens Park, South Australia 5062
0800 222 062
e-mail: info@hknewzealand.com

E5595

CONTENTS

ACKNOWLEDGEMENTS

We would like to acknowledge the very keen interest of the teachers and children of the grade three/four classes at Roberts McCubbin Primary School in Melbourne, Australia, who wholeheartedly immersed themselves in creative PE. These children and their teachers worked through their own creative PE project, adapting it to their needs and circumstances. The children who appear in the photographs throughout this book are specifically from class 3/4A. We thank them and their families for permission to use photographs of them at work (or should we say play). We would also like to specifically thank Meg Alexander for her support as teacher advocate of creative PE at this school.

Additionally we would like to highlight the input of staff at Human Kinetics who have supported us through the process of bringing these ideas to publication—and thus sharing them beyond the immediate worlds we inhabit. The book has been enhanced by their creative efforts.

We have called this book *Creative Physical Education* because we wish to emphasize what sits at the heart of physical education: the creative work of teachers and students. Physical education is not about mimicking and repeating what adults already know; rather, it involves students and teachers in a creative enterprise in which acquiring and practising new knowledge and skills are key to meaningful achievements.

The achievements we speak of are encompassed within the innovative project that characterises creative PE. The new knowledge and skill required to achieve the creative PE project is primarily in physical education, but drawing too tight a boundary around subjects means that important learning opportunities can be overlooked. For this reason, creative PE is best supported by integrating curriculum.

Creative PE is, in simple terms, a class project in physical education. But we are using the term *project* in a particular way, distancing it from a focus on a certain topic and instead emphasizing engagement at a more personal level.

As a class project, creative PE involves multiple inquiries into multiple topics, all connected by engagement with actually *being* a teammate. This is the basic challenge: creating a successful team. Teammates face the challenge of, as a *team,* creating a *game* to play in a season of games, creating a *season* that incorporates

Students engaged in a creative PE project have roles as team members, game designers, players and umpires.

multiple opportunities for improvement, and creating the ways in which the team will *practise* to achieve this improvement. These four elements of team, game, season and practice form the structure of this teacher's guide and student workbook. Chapter 1 focuses on creating teams. Chapter 2 leads teams through the process of creating games that will evolve to become the one class game. Chapter 3 outlines how to create a seasonal structure for playing the game that the class has created. Finally, chapter 4 explores ways in which the teams can be involved in creating practice activities that will help them to improve their playing of this game. These four chapters constitute the teacher's guide that assists you in planning your version of a creative PE project. The student workbook that follows the teacher's guide includes the forms that each student will need while participating in the project. These forms should be adapted for your purposes and then duplicated and collated into a workbook for each student in your class. Alternatively, these forms could exist in their electronic form and students could complete them on computer, building an electronic portfolio. A CD-ROM that includes all forms is bound into this text so that you may easily access, customize and print these forms for your students.

Creative Physical Education is most appropriate for students from middle primary years to middle secondary years, or between the ages of 7 and 16. In this age range children and young adolescents are generally more attuned to the issue of who they are and how they belong. With this in mind, the book embraces the broad interests of young people in social physical activity. In this way, creative PE is student-centered, but the leader of this project is always the teacher.

It is expected that you, the teacher, will customize a creative PE project for your class, meaningfully integrating aspects of the broader curriculum into achievement of the project. We have incorporated possible curriculum integration opportunities throughout the text as well as presenting in an appendix an overview of curriculum concerns in various countries.

The commentary we provide in the teacher's guide is illustrated with thumbnail pages from the student workbook. These forms are available on the accompanying CD in a format that will enable you to customize them to your needs. In general, the student forms have been written in language appropriate to middle-to-upper primary school children. This was done with the understanding that it is sometimes easier to write for older children than for younger, so we took it upon ourselves to deal with the more difficult end of the language spectrum. We expect that secondary school teachers would manipulate the language on these pages to accommodate their students where necessary.

One other way we have tried to help in the teacher's guide is by highlighting suggestions at appropriate points throughout *Creative Physical Education* where, from our experience, teachers have had to think a little bit harder about the logistics of the process.

Team

Game

Season

Practice

CREATING TEAM, GAME, SEASON AND PRACTICE

Being a teammate is at the heart of creative PE. But a team needs a game and a season as well as opportunities for practice. Creative

PE engages each *team* and each teammate in the development of a class *game* that will be played throughout a *season* where the emphasis is on improvement via *practice* during the season.

Introduce creative PE to students with an overview of creating team, game, season and practice. Students need to understand the entire project from the beginning. They need to understand where the project is going, where they will end up and who they are being asked to be. In this way the project becomes meaningful to them, and they can get a broad sense of the expectations, of what is required and of the challenges that await them.

A creative PE project is not a small undertaking. We suggest running it as an integrated unit, possibly spanning a term; if conducted just once a week, it may require half a year of work. The first half of the project encompasses issues of team and the creation of the class game. The second half involves the teams playing this class game for a season, providing lots of opportunities for practice. See table I.1.

ASSESSMENT

Creative PE has not been designed with any formal assessment attached to it although this could readily be undertaken if so desired. Instead, it is anticipated that teachers will grasp the many opportunities for formative assessment that structure a creative PE project, opportunities that encourage continuous evaluation of students using the evidence collected in the student workbook.

Many of the achievements students make by way of their participation in the project support the broad range of skills and knowledge that are taught daily in the classroom. A creative PE project offers opportunities for student growth in numerous curriculum areas, thus providing teachers with evidence of learning beyond physical education. It is for this reason that we present creative PE as an integrated inquiry.

Some of the deepest and richest learning that occurs during a creative PE project will be best perceived through analysis of teacher observations; thus, monitoring students in a targeted way as well as keeping anecdotal records are useful means of collecting evidence. Some teachers may wish to create and use rubrics for assessment purposes. We

Table I.1 Two Possible Halves of a Creative PE Project

FIRST HALF Teams creating the game		SECOND HALF Teams playing the season	
Lesson 1 60 mins	Announce teams What is a team? Levels role play 1 What is a game? Levels record	Lesson 1 60 mins	Practice games What is practice? Teamwork Levels record
Lesson 2 90 mins	Levels role play 2 Create a game Share games Review games Levels record	Lesson 2 90 mins	Season game 1 Teamwork Fitness practice Levels record
Lesson 3 90 mins	Levels role play 3 Improve game Share games Review games Levels record	Lesson 3 90 mins	Season game 2 Teamwork Skills practice Levels record
Lesson 4 90 mins	Levels role play 4 Improve game Share games Review games Levels record	Lesson 4 90 mins	Season game 3 Teamwork Strategy practice Levels record
Lesson 5 60 mins	Class game draft 1 Class game review Levels record	Lesson 5 60 mins	Season game 4 Team practice Levels record
Lesson 6 60 mins	Class game draft 2 Class game review Levels record	Lesson 6 60 mins	Season game 5 Team practice Levels record
Lesson 7 60 mins	Class game draft 3 Class game review Levels record	Lesson 7 60 mins	Season game 6 Team practice Levels record
Lesson 8 60 mins	Class game draft 4 Class game review Levels record	Lesson 8 60 mins	Finals games Team practice Levels record
Lesson 9 60 mins	Class game final What is a season? Levels record	Lesson 9 60 mins	Finals games Levels record Celebration

have not provided these. We appreciate that they are best designed for particular settings and with an understanding of how your students will approach the tasks.

BRINGING TOGETHER DIFFERENT MODELS OF PHYSICAL EDUCATION

Creative Physical Education brings together aspects of models important in the teaching of physical education. The model described in Hellison's (2010) *Teaching Personal and Social Responsibility Through Physical Activity* is crucial in relation to team membership. This model enables a teacher to scaffold student understanding of what it means to be a teammate by providing a ladder of teammate levels that students set out to climb, both individually and together, because climbing this ladder means that the team will improve. It also sets clear expectations for behavior, an important component of managing a class through the interpersonal challenges of a creative PE project.

Student-Designed Games (Hastie, 2010) is another model we adapt and integrate within *Creative Physical Education*. This model has been discussed for many years (Almond, 1983; Curtner-Smith, 1996). Here we take it a step further by distinguishing the ingredients of games, those structural aspects that need to be considered when creating a game. By working with these ingredients, teachers can build upon students' game-making efforts, set relevant parameters around the design of the game and involve students in the provision of structured feedback.

Siedentop's *Sport Education* (1994) emphasizes the major characteristics of sport that we employ, including team affiliation and competition. This model highlights how sport is more than specific sports, and it identifies the structures of sport in general, similar to the ingredients for games. However, we differ somewhat in our employ of the diverse roles that structure sport, preferring for these roles to be taken on by the team as a whole, rather than specified individuals. When games are played at recess or lunch time, everyone is involved in refereeing, scoring, coaching, managing, and so on. By adapting this model of play for the project, everyone can learn and be involved with these roles without having to stop playing.

Teaching Games for Understanding (Butler & Griffin, 2010; Griffin & Butler, 2005; Werner, Thorpe & Bunker, 1996) is a model that critically informs the practice phase of creative PE, which is conducted throughout the season. This model emphasizes the learning of strategies and tactics of the game, along with the necessary development of motor skills and techniques. The focus on techniques in isolation of game play is often identified as a problem with models that highlight fundamental movement skills alone. The bringing together of game sense and technical ability (tactics and strategies combined with techniques and skills) is also the premise of *Play Practice* (Launder & Piltz, 2001). Another aspect of *Teaching Games for Understanding* is the stress placed on student-centered pedagogy, which aligns well with the conduct of creative PE.

In addition to tactics, strategies, techniques and skills, the practice phase of creative PE is concerned with health-related fitness, especially as this involves improvements in cardiorespiratory endurance, muscular endurance, strength and flexibility—or in language more familiar to young people: fitness, strength and flexibility. We interpret these more specifically in terms of game-related fitness, to maintain connection with the most tangible goals of the project.

However, this brief overview cannot convey the subtle detail of how these models come together in *Creative Physical Education* nor of how students and teacher are co-involved in a creative PE project. We present this detail for you, the teacher, in this book. Each phase of a creative PE project—team, game, season and practice—is explained for you here, via our commentary. Creative PE is designed to be supported in practice by the student workbook. This provides a coherent structure for each phase of the project as it unfolds in practice, thereby supporting the collaborative development of ideas and the recording of information that can assist the teacher in monitoring each student's and each team's progress. We repeat that the language used in the student workbook pages is targeted at middle-upper primary school students, so it may need to be manipulated for secondary school students. The student workbook pages are available on the accompanying CD in a format that can be easily customised.

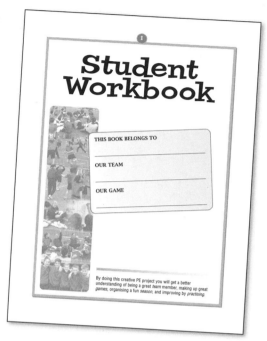

We want to emphasize that creative PE is student-centered; however this does not mean that the teacher is superfluous, with the students making all the decisions. The teacher's role in a creative PE project is central. The teacher initiates the project, designing and customizing it to best suit the young people in the class and school. The teacher sets out the path the students will follow and guides them along it, teaching explicitly where necessary. This is a path, a journey, a curriculum designed to be meaningful to them here and now, not in some remote adult future. In this way, what the students learn in the project can be encountered in a living context where it has genuine meaning.

SUMMARY

With this introduction we have tried to position the broad ideas behind *Creative Physical Education* for you. There are many aspects to it, but creative PE is fundamentally about making PE meaningful for all students, not just those who play competitive sport. In fact it is the very competitive athlete, most used to just being a game player in PE, who often finds the transition to creative PE the most challenging. Creative PE is not just about playing the game, it is about creating your team, creating the game, creating a season and creating practice activities. In making these claims for creative PE, we hope that we have whet your appetite and that you are ready and willing to learn more. The following chapters adhere to the structure of a creative PE project: creating team, game, season, practice. We wish you the very best in your explorations of this way of thinking about and teaching PE and hope that at some stage you may find the time to adapt it to your circumstances and give it a go.

PART I

TEACHER'S GUIDE

CHAPTER 1

Team

▶ **The Striking Vipers.**

The *team* is the heart of a creative PE project. The school class of approximately 20 to 30 students is carefully divided into four permanent teams. The teacher works with the class, organised in these teams, for the entire unit. Thus the teams are ongoing work groups. While some may think that this does not give students an opportunity to work with other people, we disagree for three reasons. We believe that having ongoing work groups facilitates the development of deeper relationships. Additionally, each team will be interacting with other teams in numerous ways. Finally, a creative PE project is just one of many things they are doing at school; there are many more opportunities for selecting groups with different student composition beyond those in creative PE.

Curriculum Integration

Mathematics (Statistics and Probability)

Students can investigate a well-known and popular sport that has a salary cap and player draft system to understand how the system works mathematically and the reason for the design.

For students, working in one team for an extended period allows for the development of a much deeper sense of belonging: Their team membership becomes very meaningful to them as they build their team, often by confronting and overcoming the disagreements and conflicts that are a natural part of life. The continuing nature of these teams enables a teaching strategy that focuses on each team becoming a really good team over time. At first, a student may ask, "Why should I do these things?" The teacher answers, "Because it is important for your team's improvement and success." As team affiliation builds, interactions between teammates will reflect the growing importance of teams, as they say to one another, "You should do this because it is important for *our* team's improvement and success." Hellison's model, which describes taking personal and social responsibility through physical activity, is very important here (2010).

TEAM SELECTION AND AFFILIATION

The selection of the teams is a task that should, in our view, be conducted by the teacher. While it would seem to be an easy task that could be managed by randomly assigning teams, or even a job that could be handed over to the students, the evenness of teams is of such importance to the ongoing success of the project that it must be done with great care. A very uneven competition can mean very unhappy teams, especially as we move into the season of games. Having said this, however, we do know of teachers who have involved the children in the team selection, but they have done this carefully over a number of classes, dealing with all of the conflicts that arise.

It is interesting to note that some sporting competitions, notably the Australian Football League, go to great lengths to achieve as even a competition as possible. Strategies such as having a salary cap and a player draft that benefits lower-placed teams help to remove the large differences that can develop between teams, as evident in the English Premier League football competition.

So we strongly suggest that you, the teacher, select the teams to ensure the greatest chance that the teams are evenly balanced in terms of gender, ability, friendships, and of course, number of team members. Usually there will be four teams of between five and eight members, depending on class size. There may be a slight unevenness in numbers between teams, but this is a normal occurrence; it will also occur

Curriculum Integration

Visual Arts

Students can investigate shields, crests and logos and the ways in which they have been designed to represent certain ideas, such as determination or friendship. They can use various media, techniques and processes to develop shields, crests or logos to communicate these ideas about their own team.

Music

Students can compose their team chants more formally with instruments and score them using standard notation. They can then be performed as a contribution to this particular music genre.

when students are absent from class. This unevenness should be taken into consideration when the game is being developed, because it is important that the game can be played fairly even if a few people are away from class on a particular day. We have found that the best way to manage uneven teams is via the design of the class game (see Uneven Numbers of Players on page 29).

The first pages of the student workbook, My Team and Team Profiles, help build a student's affiliation with the team. A possible adaptation here is completing these pages as posters to be displayed. Notably, this sense of team affiliation is a central characteristic of the sport education model. The teacher should take a photo of each team and print copies that can be pasted in the workbook by the students and labeled with each team member's name. At this time, each team should begin discussing their team name. This can be a difficult process for some teams, and it may take a few weeks to sort out. There is no immediate rush to have a team name although it must be decided before the season begins. Developing a team chant is something that could be done in class when there is a spare moment between other lessons, or for homework. The chant can be very simple, but it must be positive and not demeaning of other teams. Drawing a team shield, crest or logo is another way in which team affiliation can be promoted.

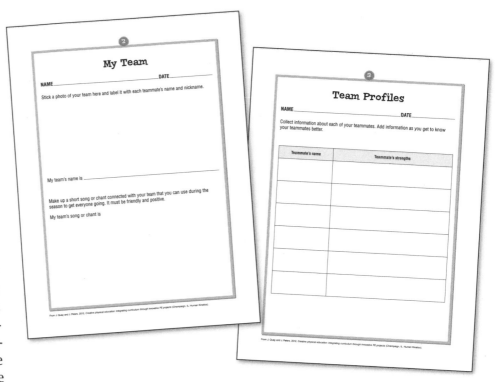

Beginning to build a profile of each team member is an exercise that can bring together students on the same team who may not previously have had much interaction at school. It can break the ice between team members. It is also an exercise that can be built on during a creative PE project as team members get to know each other better. The questions posed in the sample workbook documents are not prescribed in any way; they are designed to be positive.

BEING A TEAMMATE

Identifying with a team by way of the My Team page and the Team Profiles begins to give students a sense of the longer term relevance of their team. Teams in physical education are often short-lived, which reduces the meaning of being a teammate. Arguments can be made for having short-lived teams so that the elements of conflict and competition are reduced, both within a team and between teams. But planning to avoid conflict and competition is not the way to teach students how to best manage situations that they will naturally confront in every sphere of life.

In order to help students develop a sense of the expectations, the teacher should begin with a collection of what we have called *supertasks*. These are age-appropriate tasks that should be designed with student creativity in mind. They should also enable integration between a creative PE project and other areas of the curriculum. We have incorporated supertasks into each phase of creative PE.

The team supertasks should have students inquiring into various aspects of what it means to be a good teammate. There are numerous ways to do this, of course; the following are some ideas. Students should be able to choose amongst these options for the supertask, deciding on one that they would most like to attempt and achieve, both in school and for homework. Alternatively, the teacher might like to prescribe a set number of tasks to be completed over a designated time and even specify one particularly relevant task as a compulsory class or team task.

The team supertasks provide a rich source of knowledge and experience that support more directed class discussion around the notion of a 'great team.' Discussion can initially occur in teams, with individuals contributing what they have learnt via their supertask as well as in other ways. 'A champion team will

Team Supertasks

▶ Do a team activity outside of school and write about the ways in which your team encourages good teamwork.

▶ Complete a four-panel cartoon that shows how teamwork can help resolve a problem.

▶ Write an acrostic poem using the word *team* to demonstrate how you feel when you are part of a team.

▶ Interview three people within your family (for instance, your brother, sister, parent or grandparent) to find out what team sports they have played in the past. Ask them to list three things they enjoyed about being part of a team.

▶ Play a board game with your family or friends in teams. List some of the positive things they say to each other as team members.

▶ Write a short imaginative story about a team, starting with the sentence stem 'If only we had worked together as a team . . .'

▶ Observe a team game played by a brother, sister, parent or friend and count the number of things people say to each other that lead to good and poor teamwork. Display this in a bar graph.

▶ Create or adapt a card game that the class could play in teams. You will need to describe and then show the class how teamwork is involved in this game.

▶ Collect examples from online or other published material of great teams or problems in teams.

▶ Explore some of the famous sayings that model the message that a good team is stronger than any individual.

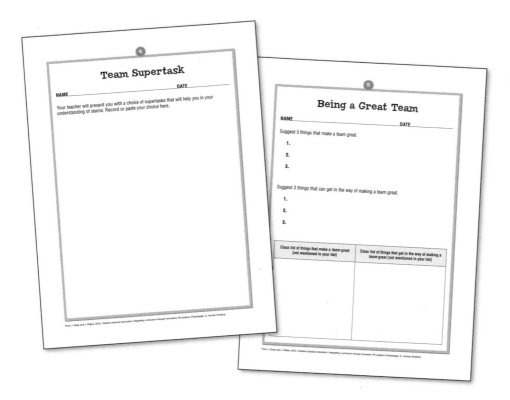

always beat a team of champions' is a statement that can engage thinking and discussion. Give each team a chance to identify three characteristics of great teams that they can list on the Being a Great Team workbook page. In addition, each team could suggest characteristics of poor teams. Each team can share their suggestions, and the whole class can develop a master list. These lists can be referred to when introducing the five teammate levels.

THE FIVE LEVELS OF BEING A TEAMMATE

After initiating discussion about the characteristics of a great team (and problems in teams), the teacher should introduce the five levels adapted from the taking personal and social responsibility in PE model (Hellison 2010). Teammates will refer to these levels when they analyse their performances as teammates throughout the entire length of a creative PE project. Connections should be made between the levels, the ideas the students have raised via their supertasks and the class lists about the qualities of being a great team.

As with every phase of creative PE, the emphasis is on improvement. Team members conduct self-assessments according to these levels at the end of every physical education class, recording their thoughts and understanding in their student workbooks. This self-assessment is completed knowing that the teacher will regularly be looking through the workbooks in order to monitor progress. A cumulative table is also available in the workbook to make this progress more visible.

As a teacher you will see the importance of students moving up the levels. But these levels are also significant to the students in relation to their teams. *These levels are important from a team perspective because the more teammates there are operating at the higher levels, the more likely it is that the team will be a great team.* That is why we refer to them as the five levels of being a teammate. They are detailed below and in figure 1.1.

- Level 0 is the lowest level; it describes a teammate who has been making it difficult for others to participate. This teammate is *disrespectful* of the team.
- Level 1 characterises a teammate who has not been very involved in the team. This teammate doesn't upset others, so basic *respect* is shown, but this person doesn't help the team.

Figure 1.1

Teammate Levels

▶ **Level 4: I was respectful, I participated, I was motivated, and I was CARING of others.**

Teammates at level 4, in addition to respecting others, participating and being motivated, take on responsibility for others by giving support, showing concern and helping.

▶ **Level 3: I was respectful, I participated, and I was MOTIVATED.**

Teammates at level 3 not only show respect for others, but they are motivated to participate without always having to be asked. However, they often do so without really thinking of their teammates.

▶ **Level 2: I was respectful and I PARTICIPATED when asked.**

Teammates at level 2 not only show respect for others but also participate when asked by other teammates or the teacher.

▶ **Level 1: I was RESPECTFUL of others.**

Teammates at level 1 may or may not participate in the activities, but they don't get in the way of the participation of other teammates.

▶ **Level 0: I was DISRESPECTFUL.**

Teammates at level 0 interfere with other teammates' participation.

The five teammate levels show the meaning of progression from level 0 to level 4.

- Level 2 characterises a teammate who has been involved in the team but only when specifically asked to do things by other teammates or the teacher. This teammate *participates* in a basic way, but only when asked to.

- The level 3 teammate is *motivated,* aware of what needs to be done for the team, and does it. But this person does not always think a lot about how others are feeling, usually thinking more about the self than others.

- The level 4 teammate is motivated and concerned about the whole team and how each teammate is feeling. This person *cares* for all teammates as well as people in other teams. In this sense, such a teammate is a team leader.

In order for these levels to function fairly, teams need to be truly democratic in nature rather than democratic in a representative sense; that is, they should not have a designated or elected captain. This provides the best opportunity for each teammate to show caring and leadership when the situation calls for it, thus moving up the levels. We think the alternative notion of sharing leadership around the team by having a different captain each week is somewhat false. In such small teams, leadership does not need to be proclaimed by a title but should be manifest in the situation.

Curriculum Integration

Civics

Students can investigate how the various principles of democracy apply not only to forms of government but also to governance in a small group setting.

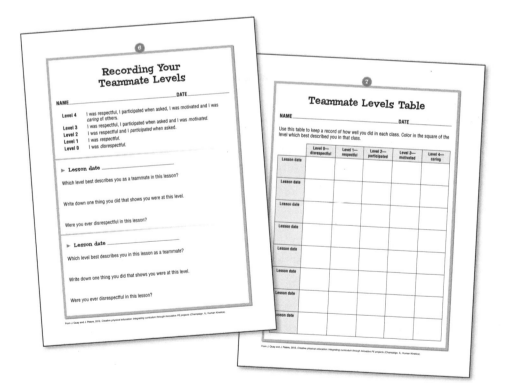

TEAMMATE ROLE PLAYS

The teacher can introduce these levels using practical activities such as role playing. The levels should not be introduced as if they need to be somehow memorized like times tables. The meaning of the levels in practice is more important than being able to recite them. Role plays do not need to take place outside (although they could) but can be run in a classroom. Each team develops a short role play that encompasses all of the levels in action. The Teammate Levels Role Play page in the student workbook helps with this task.

While a team is performing their role play, other teams are watching and trying to determine which person in the performing team is operating at which level. The performance can be repeated if necessary. Each observing team is then asked to discuss the performance and come to an agreement about who was at what level and why they thought so. The Teammate Levels Discussion page will help facilitate this. The outcome of these discussions is then shared by each team with the class. This provides the teacher with an opportunity to expand on the definitions of each level in practice, helping the students

---

Curriculum Integration

Civics and History

Students can investigate the importance of mateship or community spirit to notions of citizenship as they have evolved over time.

The more teammates who are operating at high levels, the more likely it is that their team will be a great one.

become familiar with their interpretations of the levels. It also assists teachers to monitor student understanding.

The four role plays, one for each team, do not need to be performed in the same lesson. Spacing them over four lessons enables you to continue highlighting the levels at the beginning of the first four lessons in a practical way, thereby reinforcing the language of the levels (see Two Possible Halves of the PE Project on page xi). It is very important that the language of the levels pervade your class as early as possible. The levels enable you to work with your class in a positive rather than disciplinary way, setting positive expectations that support you as teacher and are also meaningful for students as teammates.

The levels do not need to be confined to physical education; they can be incorporated into other aspects of life in school. However, from a physical education perspective, the levels will allow you as teacher to conduct games or lessons without needing to umpire or referee; rather, you can manage the class as a whole while teams simultaneously play multiple games.

In the next chapter, we discuss the student creation and design of their own team games. This is the next phase of creative PE.

Curriculum Integration

Performing Arts

Students can be asked to create characters, environments and actions by writing short scripts, using props and rehearsing.

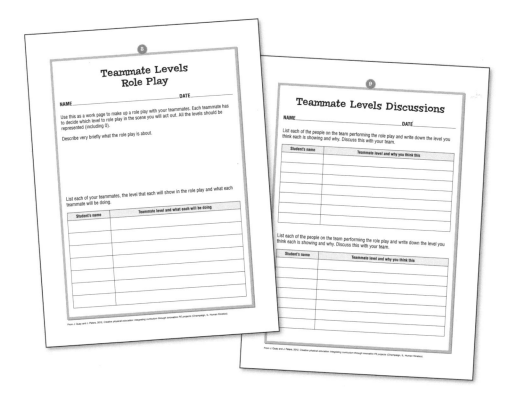

CHAPTER 2

Game

▶ The Funky Monkeys.

We are now moving on to discuss creating and designing games but must stress again that the team is at the heart of creative PE. The teams are centrally involved in creating and designing a team game, and the nature of this involvement contributes to the eventual design of the class game used through the season. We never leave behind the team issues and the levels. The levels records are used throughout the whole project.

The first major activity challenge for the teams is to create and design a game—a game that will contribute to the ultimate goal of having a single class game for a season of games. This creation and design task is organised so that each team can provide and receive feedback from other teams, a process that takes a number of lessons (see Two Possible Halves of a Creative PE Project on page xi of the introduction).

The process is structured so that each team shares its work with each other team over a series of lessons (for instance, team A shares with team B, and team

Curriculum Integration

Health (Relationships and Communication)

Students should demonstrate negotiation skills and strategies to manage conflict (such as mediation) within the framework of the teammate levels. These skills and strategies should be investigated and employed to structure dispute resolution.

C with team D; then A-C, B-D and so forth). It involves designing, teaching, playing, reviewing and then repeating the entire process. Such sharing highlights the importance of being able to communicate with peers. *This is a time when activities can be introduced that focus on positive and clear communication.* One such activity involves students in pairs, back to back, having to communicate ideas without being able to see the other or what that person may be describing. Another activity has students passing information in whispers along a line—the grapevine. Both activities highlight how easy it is for communication to go astray and the care that must be taken to avoid misunderstandings.

Each team develops a game to teach to another team and play with that team until the other team understands how it works. Through a structured review, the other team provides feedback that teams will use in the next lesson as a basis for further improving the game. Over three or more lessons, each team will teach versions of its game to every other team while learning various versions of the other teams' games, giving and receiving feedback along the way.

After this round robin, there will be four team games. It is then the teacher's role to facilitate a move from these four games to the one class game for use in the season. The teams should be made aware of this eventual move from four games to one before they begin to create their games.

We do acknowledge that some teachers will not have time to extend creative PE into a season in the way to be shown. In this circumstance we highlight again the flexibility available within creative PE. A possible adaptation to consider is playing another round robin series involving teaching and learning of games, but this time scoring each game. Such scoring can be compiled to record team improvement. As there will be less time focused on game creation and review, there will be more time to focus on skills, tactics and other elements of team performance in the latter half of the lesson. The important point here is that the skills prescribed by the teacher have been incorporated in all four games, and so improvement in these skills is meaningful because it is a significant part of improving team performance. In a similar way fairly generic strategies can be discussed that improve performance in all games.

WHAT IS A GAME?

Coming up with a game for students is traditionally considered the teacher's responsibility. The teacher also normally picks the teams, teams that will probably only be together for this one lesson. The teacher also acts as the umpire or referee during the game, making it very difficult to do anything else. Even if students are involved in making up a game, this is often only a fun sideline, with the games they create going no further than one or two lessons.

To find appropriate games, teachers may search through books and websites and ask friends and colleagues. They may adapt games they hear about or see. Over the long term, they develop a repertoire of games that they keep up their sleeves, knowing which games may suit different age levels and how to adapt them.

But there is another way of understanding and working with games. Rather than believing that it is solely the teacher's responsibility to create the game, students can be meaningfully involved in this process. Many, if not most, children and young adolescents are continually involved in creating games during recess and lunchtimes, before and after school or on weekends. It is these occasions that we believe physical education should influence. Physical education is not just about physical activity (if it were, we would just run the students ragged for their time in PE class), and it is not just about teaching for involvement in adult sports (where much of the organisation is dependent on adults). Physical education should be about educating young people so that they are well equipped to take advantage of occasions for social physical activity outside of the physical education class. This means they need to understand how teams work, how games work, how seasons work and how practice works (which is another way of saying how to improve). They can then bring their own creativity to these opportunities that exist outside PE.

In the team phase of creative PE, we introduced supertasks. We can use *game* supertasks to get students thinking and discussing the issues surrounding

Game Supertasks

▶ Interview your parents and grandparents, asking them about some of the games they played at recess and lunchtime when they were at school. You may not have heard of some of them! Record the conversation so you can listen to it again later.

▶ Write a short story about learning a new game for the first time. Start with the stem 'It was no good. I didn't think I would ever be able to . . .'

▶ Play a game of your choice at home with a parent or sibling. List the rules that you use to help keep the game fair and explain why the rules are important.

▶ Create a game using one piece of equipment. This activity needs to have rules and, if you want, a way of scoring. You must be able to teach this game to someone else in the class.

▶ Choose one sport that you know and list all of the skills you think a player needs to be able play the game properly.

▶ List all of the games you can think of that can be played outdoors in the school grounds (not sports). Find some way of categorizing these games.

▶ Cut an article out of the newspaper about a sport you don't know very well. Paste it in your workbook. Describe the rules and how the game is scored.

▶ Imagine a game that hasn't been invented yet but might be played in the year 2200. Draw a player from that game including the special equipment necessary for playing the game. Label your diagram. Try to imagine what technology might have been invented by then!

▶ Create a rhyming poem about games. Make it four lines. Think about what fun games can be.

▶ Think of a game you know in which changes should be made to the way it is played. Draft a letter to the organisers about how you think it could be changed and why you have made those suggestions.

▶ In games there are always winners and losers. Cut out of a newspaper examples of a good winner and loser and a bad winner and loser. These might be news stories or you might find pictures that can tell a story!

games. The game supertasks should have students inquiring into various aspects of what a game is. Following are some ideas for these. Students should be able to choose amongst these options for the supertask that they would most like to attempt and achieve, both in school and for homework. These ideas further reveal how a creative PE project can be integrated with other curriculum areas beyond physical education.

Like the team supertasks, the game supertasks provide a rich source of knowledge and experience that supports more directed class discussion around the notion of a great game. Discussion can initially occur in teams, with individuals contributing what they have learnt via their supertask as well as other ways. Give each team a chance to identify three characteristics of great games that they can list on the Making a Great Game page. In addition, each team could suggest things that get in the way of making a game great. Each team can share its suggestions and help develop class lists. These lists can be recorded by the teacher (e.g., by taking a photo of the class board) and referred to when introducing the ingredients that need to be used when the students create and design their great game.

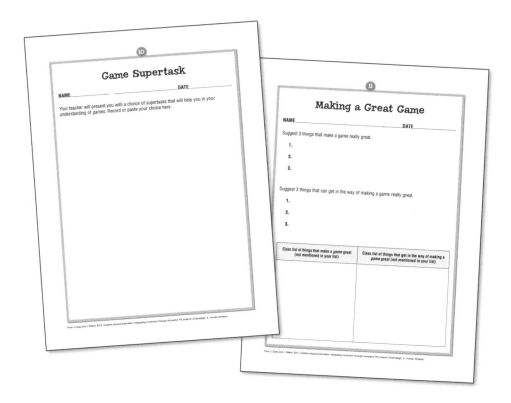

THE INGREDIENTS OF GAMES

Involving young people in creating and designing games must be done in a way that allows them to genuinely contribute. Giving students only a short time to create a game, without an understanding of the ingredients they must combine in order to do so, and without an avenue for gaining constructive feedback, makes it a very difficult task—one that rarely results in an appropriate game. However, if the ingredients are understood, and sufficient time and relevant feedback can be provided, then a great game can be cooked up!

The ingredients for making up a game can seem obvious when we list them, but being aware of these ingredients allows the teacher to structure and organise the game creation and design process so that students have a good sense of what is expected.

- Every game has a level of *enjoyment.*
- Every game has a level of *participation.*
- Every game has a level of *safety.*
- Every game requires *skills.*
- Every game has *equipment.*
- Every game has a period of *time.*
- Every game has a *space.*
- Every game has a method for *umpiring or refereeing.*
- Every game has a method for *scoring.*

Take time to teach the ingredients of games so that students have a good sense of what is expected.

We need to think about all of these ingredients when we create a game. But in the physical education setting, it is the teacher who determines the broad parameters surrounding each ingredient, parameters that guide the students in their game creation.

Enjoyment

A game must be enjoyable. This may seem so blatantly obvious that it does not merit mentioning. However, when it comes to providing and receiving feedback, this ingredient can be crucial, shedding light on how other teams perceive a game. People's preferences will rarely be identical. Attending to this ingredient means attending to the likes and dislikes of different people in the class. It may also help to raise discussion around other issues of difference such as gender and physical ability.

Participation

Enjoyment of a game is often related to levels of participation. If the game requires people who make errors to be excluded from the game for significant periods of time, then the level of participation for these people will be low, and they will be less likely to enjoy the game. Paradoxically, it is the students who are making errors that we as teachers want to see having the most activity time. We prefer a game that does not involve people 'going out.' If the game requires people who make errors to stop playing, this must only be for a very short time, with some mechanism available for quickly returning them to the game.

Young people are very aware of these issues of participation and can manipulate them to their own advantage if not guided by the teacher. But with guidance, students are quite capable of designing a game that takes into consideration the situation of every person in the class, thus enabling everyone to participate. This guidance can take the form of questions and suggestions from the teacher monitoring each team as it continues to improve its game. Young people with disabilities can be thoroughly included in the games that they help to create and design with others in their class. The game is not adapted for differences but built from scratch to include everyone. This often opens up great opportunities for students to learn more about each other.

Safety

Enjoyment and participation cannot be disconnected from safety in all its forms: physical, social and emotional. Probably the first point to discuss in relation to safety is the space that is being used. Being aware of physical hazards such as nearby walls and poles, and taking any action deemed necessary in order to minimize these dangers, provides valuable learning. Even the basic step of regularly inspecting for debris, water or other surface irregularities can make a difference to everyone's well-being.

Of course the way the game is designed will also affect safety. There are many factors to consider, but safety can be increased or decreased with simple rule changes in a game. Because the game must support a high level of participation from everyone in the class, it must feel safe to everyone in the class. The key is awareness of safety as an issue so that it is discussed when the games are being designed. The teacher can always step in and request a change in the design of a game when it can be seen to involve unsafe actions. Students are quite capable of recognizing unsafe situations, especially when safety is made an explicit ingredient for the game.

These unsafe situations also, of course, involve consideration of emotional and interpersonal safety. Students should feel that the game is safe in all ways, not just physically. Safety in this sense concerns not only the game rules, but the way the game is played between teams. It is important that the teammate levels be applied to all who are playing the game.

Skills

From the beginning of the process of creating and designing the game, the teacher is thinking about the motor skills the students should be developing and demonstrating. These are incorporated from the start by asking the students to include them as specific ingredients of the game.

We advocate showing students these skills in their basic form and then having them try the skills in a limited way so that everyone has an understanding of the expectations and the terms being used. But this way of approaching skill development is very different to the more traditional method of focusing on a skill and practicing it before using it in some form of game. In creative PE, we are not proposing that mastery of skill occur before the game is played. Rather we emphasize team, game and season as the reasons for wanting to master the skill during the season's practice opportunities.

Skill testing of individual students can always occur during creative PE, but this should happen in the background and emphasize improvement, rather than being simply summative assessment tasks. Better still, the teacher could be monitoring individual students when they are using these skills in context (rather than in a contrived testing situation): while they are playing games.

Equipment

Having decided upon the skills to be developed and included in the game, and having become aware of issues of enjoyment, participation and safety, the teacher can now determine the equipment to be used by each team. Each team has an identical set of equipment to use. Identical items but different colors for each team helps; this makes it easier for teams to take responsibility for their equipment. It may also play a part in the team names that are developed.

Not all the equipment provided needs to be used, and, since teams know what equipment is available for each team, they can access the other team's equipment as well as their own. This reduces the complexity of the task for both students and teacher and enables easier sharing and management of equipment.

Throwing is a skill that contributes to success in many types of games.

The equipment should be selected based on the skills being developed. For example, if a prescribed skill involves throwing, catching or kicking of some sort, then balls that are the size, softness, shape and texture appropriate to the age group should be provided. The number of balls should at least equal the number of students in each team so that everyone can be hands-on when the game is being designed. It also means that when students begin to develop practice games and drills later on, everyone can be involved.

Other useful equipment includes cones, spot markers, beanbags, flat hoops and bibs or sashes. These should also be provided in quantities equal to the number of team members. While this equipment may seem simplistic and perhaps oriented to younger students, it is amazing to witness the creative ways in which teams put it to use. Young people seem much more capable of thinking laterally in relation to the meaningful use of these things than many adults.

You will notice that a creative PE project can be conducted with equipment that is generally available to most schools. There is no need for very specialized equipment, which is often expensive and beyond the reach of some schools.

Time

Time is a central consideration for many games, especially if a time constraint is used to signal the end of the game. This particular constraint is not necessary for the games the students create since they may decide that the game concludes when one team achieves some task before the other team. However, the eventual class game should be relatively short in duration, and it should include some opportunity (perhaps a half-time break), for each team to meet before the end of the game to talk tactics and organise immediate improvements to the way they are playing.

The relatively short duration of the eventual class game may mean five-minute halves for younger children, gradually increasing as the student age increases, but still remaining shorter than adult games. This constraint will keep the games short and sharp and thus vigorous. But it also allows time for practice during the lessons through the season, so it is related to the length of the lesson in total. During the season, the game would be played first, and then practices organised around performance issues.

We repeat here that we do not consider physical education lessons to be where young people achieve all of their physical activity. PE should provide some of this, but it should empower young people to organise their own social physical activity in the opportunities that exist outside physical education class, such as recess and lunchtimes, before and after school, and on weekends and through holidays. This would ideally occur in addition to the adult organised sports that some students are involved with.

Space

Some schools are blessed with large grounds and many options for playing space, indoor and outdoor; others are very constrained in terms of space, especially inner-city primary schools. Most commonly, we have conducted creative PE projects on outdoor basketball courts although this may not be a big enough space for older students in large classes.

The court, or whatever space you are using, is divided into four equal planning spaces, one for each team. The teams should know that this is planning space only, and that when they play their game with another team, they will be using the other team's space as well. This means that the total space should be able to accommodate two games being played at the same time. On one basketball court with younger children this usually means playing across the court, width-ways. Teams will likely be in different halves of the court from lesson to lesson, as they play different teams.

Umpiring and Refereeing

It is crucial that the games, and especially the eventual class game, are playable without a specific umpire or referee. This is how students usually set up their games during recess and lunch times. In a creative PE project everyone is referee: everyone knows the rules and maintains them. This can be achieved by calling or otherwise signaling a halt to the game if a query arises so that the issue can be resolved, as it would happen during recess and lunch time games. Here the teammate levels are an asset for the teacher and the students. The aim should be to have everyone working at levels 3 and 4.

From the perspective of umpiring and refereeing, it is also worth considering the complexity of the rules of the game. A game that has too many subtle rules is difficult to monitor and a recipe for conflict. The design of the class game must be such that making decisions about rule infringements is relatively easy.

Designing a game that is able to be umpired by the students playing the game is crucial from a pedagogical perspective because it enables the teacher to do things other than umpire. The teacher now has the capacity to monitor the learning

Because the team acts as referees, the teacher is able to monitor learning and provide feedback, support and guidance, even with multiple games going on at once.

progress of individual students and to intervene in a supportive manner when and where necessary.

This ingredient also highlights a difference between creative PE and sport education in the employ of roles. In creative PE the umpire or referee role is not taken on by an individual. Instead everyone involved in playing the game has responsibility for this task all the time. This is the same with scoring.

Scoring

The games need to be designed so that there is a clear result, although the occasional draw is acceptable. Like umpiring, the scoring for the game should be simple so that players can manage it without needing input from the teacher or other external scorekeeper. Thus the arithmetic required during a game should not be too challenging, and the score should be announced loudly and agreed to regularly.

The scoring may be as simple as one team completing a task before another team. However if goals are to be scored during a game, the parameters of a successful goal need to be obvious; for example, a cone needs to be knocked down, or a beanbag must land in a hoop. Designing a game in this way makes managing the scoring much easier and avoids conflicts.

THE CHALLENGES OF CREATING AND DESIGNING GAMES

Involving students in creating and designing games in this way often involves a change from the way they generally perceive physical education. This change means that it will take students a few lessons before they more fully comprehend what you, as teacher, wish them to do, especially in relation to creating and designing games. *It is helpful here to introduce the ingredients of games in a basic and practical way, rather than jumping right into it.* This can be achieved by first playing simple games like tag and then analyzing them in relation to the ingredients. These simple games could even be card games or board games. Another option is for the teacher to assign one very simple and not too perfect game to each team. Each team must then analyze its game according to the ingredients and work to improve it.

Getting the Creative Juices Flowing

One of the early traps that students (and teachers) fall into during this process of game creation is *talking too much.* The best way for game creation to unfold is to try out ideas that emerge. But this does not mean talking it over until the best idea finally appears. The teams, in their quarter of the space and with their bag of equipment, should try out the first idea that emerges. It is much easier to suggest adaptations to what is being tried out in practice than to be involved in relatively abstract discussions of games conducted with little actual play. The key is to get students actively trying out and adapting ideas in concrete play, manipulating the equipment and maneuvering players in the space through suggestions to the team. This fits with their expectation that physical education will involve activity, but it also challenges them to creatively and critically think, which some will find unusual for PE. *Explicit teaching in the development of appropriate questions and reasoned arguments can be very helpful here.*

These game creation sessions can be intense, asking students to put their ideas up amongst peers with the possibility that they will be shot down in flames. These sessions involve all the politics of the peer group; they involve disagreements as well as agreements. This intensity can lead to some students opting out, not because they are disinter-

Students work out who agrees with an idea (or not!).

ested, but because they are finding the process overwhelming. This is another reason to select your teams carefully in order to support students by reducing the social and political challenges they may face although these will still be present. The teammate levels play an important role here, and maintaining the levels records at the end of each lesson is critical. Teachers should provide a clear structure for these discussions, at least in the early lessons when the process is often most fraught and the teams and games are still in their infancy.

The relatively small numbers in teams make it easier to manage the game creation process, but there will inevitably still be issues. One of these will most likely be the domination of a team by one or two team members. One way to partially overcome this may be via the use of a talking stick (or other object) that must be held when speaking. This makes domination or lack of involvement more obvious to everyone. It also means that only one person will be speaking at a time. Introduce this concept with an activity. For example, with students sitting in a circle, one person holds an object (such as a soft toy) and calls a student's name before throwing it to the named person. This continues until all students have had at least one turn. You can introduce another soft object to make the game more complex. Names must always be called. Monitoring of the situation is crucial here: The teacher should regularly visit with each team, observing, asking for input from those they know are quieter and making suggestions to keep things moving in an appropriate direction.

As the games begin to take shape, students in their teams can draw a diagram of their game, a working blueprint. We have found that having small handheld

A small whiteboard can be very handy when discussing how a game works and trying to suggest improvements.

Curriculum Integration

Mathematics (Measurement and Geometry)

Students can measure the playing area and draw it to scale, using concepts such as perimeter and area. This can be achieved by first estimating the dimensions of the field. Then students can measure it using a range of techniques, for example, stepping one foot in front of another, striding out the area, or using a meter ruler, a measuring tape or a trundle wheel. How close were the estimates to the measurements? This information can be recorded permanently on team whiteboards as a template.

whiteboards, possibly a bit bigger than A3 size, helps a lot in this process; the team can gather around the whiteboard to discuss the drawing. If the whiteboard is magnetic, students can use the magnets as representatives of players and their movements.

Teaching Your Game to Another Team

The next challenge in this process of game creation and design is for a team to teach their developing game to another team and, in turn, to learn that other team's game. In the first cycle of this round robin process, the games will be incomplete and imperfect. But the aim is to get some feedback from another team and to then be able to continue to improve the game.

Teaching a developing game to another team raises issues similar to those experienced when making the game. There needs to be some organisation around who will speak. And because this task will occur a number of times over the next few lessons, the team can determine an order for who will lead this task for each lesson, thereby sharing responsibility. There also needs to be some consideration of how this task should be approached. We suggest the following process for teaching the teams how to teach their game. Students can introduce this process by teaching board games to each other. It doesn't matter if others already know the game; the important part of the activity is to employ the process.

1. Lay out the field with the equipment in its correct place for the game (can also be shown on whiteboard diagram).
2. Communicate the overall aim of the game: what you have to do to score.
3. Point out the names of the various positions on the field and place some people in these positions to demonstrate.
4. State what players in their positions *can* do.
5. State what players in their positions *cannot* do.
6. Demonstrate your game.

When teaching PE games amongst teams, the use of team whiteboards can also be helpful. The other team should be encouraged to ask questions, but the talking should not go on for too long. It is better to organise a practice game wherein the level of the other team's comprehension of the game will become more obvious, and specific clarifications can then be provided. This practice game should continue until the other team thinks they have a good handle on the game. The students can play the game, but they do not have to play it to its

Demonstrate to the other team what they must do to score.

completion. They need only play until each team has a score. By this time all members of both teams should have a relatively good understanding of the game.

Because the game is only in an early stage of development, there will be problems with it. Safety is the main concern, so the teacher should be carefully watching both games and intervening to either change the rules to remove the unsafe practices, or halt the game entirely—back to the drawing (white) board. Halting the game is serious, but it should rarely occur because the teacher should be monitoring each team's creation and design deliberations and be able to intervene with suggestions before the game is shared with another team.

Once this developing game has been played so that everyone has a basic understanding of it, play can be stopped. Now it is time to exchange roles and teach your game or learn the other team's game. This teaching and learning of games would occur for all four teams simultaneously in the one lesson, such as A-B and C-D in their respective halves of the total playing space.

Reviewing the Other Team's Game

After the teams in their pairs (A-B or C-D) have played both of their developing games, they will most likely be aware of problems with the other team's game (as well as with their own). Whilst each team could separately discuss the problems with their own game, this discussion would benefit from input from the other team. However, providing and receiving this feedback offers another political challenge to the teams. To avoid having teams do this face-to-face, our reviewing process has the teams swap their workbooks so that they write the review of the other team's game in the other team's books. If not using the forms as a hard copy book, this feedback could be written on a team whiteboard and

Teams discuss what feedback to provide about other teams' games.

then photographed by the teacher. It should be impressed on the students that for feedback to be best received, it should be written in a caring and constructive way.

The game review follows the structure of the ingredients of the game. A team should discuss the review together and write down their agreed responses. This can, of course, be much more easily completed in a classroom, sitting at tables arranged for each team; there is no need to stay outside to do this, though it's certainly an option. Another helpful suggestion is to brainstorm with the class a list of comments or sentence stems peers might use to give feedback about a game to another team. Focusing on positive and constructive comments, highlight the types of statements the class agrees upon as acceptable in giving feedback.

As each team works through a review of the other team's game—enjoyment, participation, safety, skills, equipment, umpire, referee and scoring—they will become more familiar with the ingredients of the game and may pick up ideas that they can incorporate into their own game. The other two ingredients (time and space) could also be incorporated into the review process, but because these are mainly set by the teacher, we have omitted them. However, the use of the available space by the game could be reflected on, especially by older students, as well as the appropriateness of the timing of the game.

The review questions are answered both qualitatively and quantitatively. We recognize that students are usually familiar with receiving numerical marks for their work, so they broadly understand what these marks mean. With only a small amount of writing to do for each ingredient, the quantitative estimation provides another quick way of communicating feedback.

GETTING TO THE ONE CLASS GAME

The teams will go through three cycles of creating and designing, then reviewing and redesigning their games. In each cycle they will share their game with a different team. Over the three cycles they will have seen every team's game in various stages of development.

The next challenge is to arrive at one class game from the four individual team games. This needs to be managed carefully by the teacher, especially considering the politics of the situation. We have learnt that the teams usually take great pride in their games; they often think their game is, if not the best, at least worthy of being used in the season, and this is often true. However, the season requires one game, so some strategy is required that will enable this issue to be worked through in a fair way, one that acknowledges the work of all the teams.

The teacher has an important role in managing the move from four team games to one class game.

The teams need to know about this need to move from four team games to one class game (to be played in the season) before they begin to create their games. It is also important for them to know that the work they are doing to create their games will, if warranted, go towards the class game. This class game will then be reviewed and further improved.

The teacher should facilitate this process from the very beginning of game creation and design. The teams should know that the teacher is looking for either a full game, or parts of games, that can be used in the class game. The teacher should take some basic notes of each team's game each week, being especially attentive to those aspects that the students seem to enjoy and that also meet the requirements emphasized via the other game ingredients.

It should be clearly stated that the teacher has ultimate responsibility for determining the class game. But this does not mean that the teacher simply makes up a game from scratch or selects one from a book. The teacher's responsibility is for the process. This may also mean playing an active role in piecing together a composite game from various parts of the four team games. We hope it is becoming obvious that there are various ways to arrive at one class game from four team games. Here are two that may work for you.

Students Prefer One of the Games

One possibility is that the teacher discovers, through informal discussions with teams, that everyone in the class prefers one particular team's game. Attempting to discover whether this is the case should never be undertaken via a whole class discussion unless the teacher is assured of the time and inclination to work through all of the political issues that may arise. We have found that because the students place great importance on their team membership and are proud of the games they have made, they are very reluctant to publicly acknowledge that their game is not as good as another team's. This means that class voting can be a very problematic strategy; it can cause some students to declare that they will not proceed with the chosen game because they do not agree with the result of the vote. At the very least, there may be unhappy and unmotivated participants with no feeling of ownership towards the new class game.

The various perceptions of the teams' games can also be gleaned from the written comments on game review sheets. Additionally, the teacher can use the game review sheets quantitatively and add up the scores for each team's game. The obvious problem with this is that the games are developing, and so problems experienced in earlier versions may have been rectified. Even so, this measure may give the teacher and students some basic ideas for making a decision.

Teacher Combines the Four Games Into One Composite Game

An additional way of moving forward is for the teacher to take those aspects of the games that meet the game design requirements and create a composite game. We have found that this strategy often works best. It mitigates the ownership issue, and at the same time it rewards teams for the work they have done. It also enables the teacher to have significant input at a crucial time, making sure that the game is fun, participatory and safe and that the skills are embedded, the equipment is used cleverly and the rules and scoring are simple. Inevitably, the style of the composite game may match one team's game more than others, but this need not be stated explicitly.

It can be quite a challenge for the teacher to come up with a composite game. It is important to begin thinking about this as soon as the team games begin to achieve some recognizable form, because it often takes time for one's thinking about a composite game to take shape. We have learnt that it pays to keep things relatively simple. Complexity can be added as the class game itself is reviewed.

Uneven Numbers of Players

An issue that must be addressed with the eventual design of the class game concerns participation when team numbers are slightly uneven. The game should be designed so that slightly uneven teams are not an issue to the fairness or integrity of the game. One way to do this is for the game to involve multiple player roles that students shift between during a game. If at least one of these roles can be performed by more than one team member simultaneously (such as two students of one team running a relay leg together or two students of one team protecting a base together), then this sharing of roles removes much of the number advantage. The composite games designed are often very interesting. Further complexity can be added by student reviews of the class game.

In the case of uneven teams, it is not appropriate to take players from a larger team and place them on the smaller team (or have someone sitting out). This undermines the meaning of being a team member! If teams are significantly uneven on any particular day because a number of students are away, and this is during the season, then the season games may have to be postponed for this lesson, and the focus placed on practice.

Reviewing the Class Game

Regardless of the way the teacher decides to arrive at one class game from four team games, a process that may involve one or a combination of the previously mentioned strategies (or a strategy that we have not considered here), this class game will still require further review by the class as they prepare for the season.

The first draft of the class game, as resolved by the teacher, should be both written and drawn using the relevant form (Our Class Game—Draft). This recording process follows the same structure used when teams were teaching their games to other teams. It specifies the overall aim of the game (or how to score), the field of equipment and the positions of players (diagram), what players can do in the various positions and what they can't do. This description and diagram can then be used by the teams to trial the game. The teacher does not necessarily have to teach the game to the class, thus avoiding the sense in students that it is the teacher's game. The team whiteboards could be very helpful here.

Reviewing this first version of the class game is important in two ways. First, the game is improved by the class, not the teacher or any specific team. This relieves some of the pressure on the teacher as the class moves from four games to one, especially if a composite game has been designed. Second, it facilitates the whole class developing ownership of this game. As all teams review and suggest improvements to this class game, it evolves as a class game rather than being one team's game. The teacher should emphasize this shift in ownership.

Game review sheets (Game Review, Game Review of Class Game) are incorporated into the student workbook so that these reviews can be discussed and recorded in a way similar to the team game reviews although teams don't need to swap books. These class game reviews, discussed and recorded by teams, can then be talked over by the whole class. All of this discussion would probably occur in the classroom, where ideas can be shared on the board. During these discussions, the need for a name for the class game can also be raised. Naming the game is another process that should help share ownership of the game across the whole class.

Following these discussions the class game can be adapted and adjusted by creating new descriptions and diagrams, this time with the direct input of the teams themselves in the wording and drawing. The new versions can then be trialed and reviewed again over a number of lessons. These discussions, leading to new descriptions and diagrams, and the additional trials and reviews, help teams become increasingly more familiar with the game, even if there are no major changes. In other words, these lessons help teach the class game to the teams. This is good preparation for the upcoming season, for which they will need to know the class game well.

Eventually, after numerous adaptations (which will have helped to shift ownership of the game to the

The class game is refined through class discussion.

class as well as improve the game), a final version of the class game can be recorded in the students' workbooks (Our Class Game—Final). Further minor adaptations may still occur during the season if all agree, but these should only be instituted if really necessary.

The class game that emerges will sometimes be an invasion type of game where scoring involves invading the other team's territory. But this is not always the case. We have witnessed younger students develop target games where each team is operating independently to knock their cones down first. We have seen students develop striking or fielding games where the strike is a kick of a ball into a field with the need to run around bases before fielders can retrieve the ball. We have even observed games with teams on opposite sides of a line, rather than a net, each trying to get balls through the other team's field placements. We have found students to be very inventive when it comes to game creation.

At last, the final version of the game is documented in the student workbook.

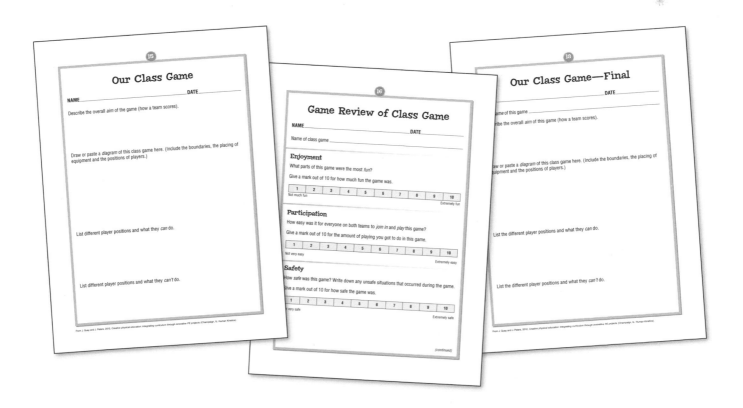

CHAPTER 3

Season

▶ The Launching Lizards.

W e now have a well-developed class game, owned and understood by every team and student in the class, to take into our season. But it is not just the game that is taken into the season. The season involves teams, so the teams are also central to the season. This means that we continue with our teammate levels records. The levels are also a crucial foundation for students being able to sort through the disagreements that will inevitably appear as they are challenged to improve their performances during the season. These disagreements will be both within and between teams. Learning how to work with others is a big part of creative PE.

FAIRNESS AND COMPETITION

A well-planned season can deliver a structure for fair competition. Both fairness and competition are required for a successful season. Yet for many teachers, *competition* is a bit of a dirty word, especially when it comes to physical education, because it can engender behaviours that are antisocial. However, we believe that in many physical education classes this is caused by a mismanagement of competition, particularly in the way competition is planned for.

Many physical education lessons do not involve ongoing teams or seasons of games. One reason for this is that some teachers believe that this way of doing things reduces competition. They believe that a season of games with the same teams will simply result in one team being successful while most others are unsuccessful. But, paradoxically, this will always be true when the 'season' is composed of only one game. When teams are only valid for one lesson and only play one game together, it may be experienced as a one-game season. The winner takes all with no chance for the losing team to improve.

In most situations, someone, some team, has to lose a game. In the situation of the one-game season, this team never gets a chance to focus that feeling of disappointment into improvement. And even if there is another game, there is not much point focusing on improvement if there is no opportunity or structure provided through which to improve. If the next physical education lesson is simply another game, then the competitive aspect is exacerbated as the losing team will most likely lose again, and so on. The one-game season only works to reduce competition because the team is less meaningful. The team lasts for only one game. So while the teacher has achieved a reduction in competition, this is done by reducing the meaning of the event for the students. They have no need to get competitive over something that means very little.

Additionally, in this circumstance, emphasis usually shifts away from the team to talented individuals. These are the players who carry the undeveloped team because they can generally perform without a team, especially when no team involved in the competition is well developed. In this form of team, there is an *I*. The game becomes a battle of the good players. Here a team of champions defeats all other teams because no other team can be a champion team. Yet these good players are not the ones who really need this high level of access to the majority of opportunities in physical education. And everyone is missing out on the learning that comes from forging a good team focused on improving across a season of games, a season that provides significant time and structure for practice.

The urge to invest in practice does not exist without the meaning provided by team, game and season. All good sporting teams spend more time practicing than playing competition games. But they practise because they are a team, the team is involved with a game, and the game is played across a season in competition with other teams. If a team loses, they look to how they can improve their performance in the next game by practicing in the interim. This is how we usually understand sport to be structured. Yet in physical education we tend to characterise sport by simply listing the names of adult sports rather than the structures that are part of all sports. These structures are well documented in the sport education model.

Season games are in full swing.

In creative PE we develop our own teams and games with a significant level of student input. These teams and games are the building blocks of sport as it is played through a season of games. It is through these structures that sport is meaningful for physical education, not just as training for adult sports. Physical education should not simply be about preparing students for adult organised sports. Physical education should help young people to understand how best to work with these structures of sport, of which a season is a major one. In the lives of many young people, informal seasons structure the playing of a game over numerous lunchtimes.

VARIOUS FORMS OF SEASON

There are many forms of season. The most common is the round robin, or versions of it, in which all teams play each other at least once. This form of season is usually perceived as fair, as long as each team plays each other team an equal number of times. Another type of season or fixture is that used in competition tennis. This is usually a knockout (or single elimination) competition that is not as fair in participatory terms as a round robin. Single elimination is structured to determine which is the best team or individual. Fairness is introduced by seeding the players and then spreading these through the draw. But in the adult world, these knockout competitions are usually part of a larger series; if you get knocked out of one, then you prepare for the next one. Still another form of season is that used in many boxing competitions, often called a challenge cup. One person or team holds the cup at any one time and others challenge this person or team; whoever wins the challenge gets to hold the cup until the next challenger comes along.

These various forms of season can be investigated with students, particularly around the issues of fairness and competition, with the aim of involving them in the decisions contributing to the structure of their season. The season super-tasks contribute to this investigation by asking students to inquire into various aspects of what a season is and how it works, including the issues of fairness and competition. There are numerous ways to do this, of course; following are some ideas. Students should be able to choose amongst these options for the supertask that they would most like to attempt and achieve, both in school and for homework.

Once the season supertasks are complete, class discussion around the notion of a 'good season' can be conducted more fruitfully. This discussion can initially occur in teams with individuals contributing what they have learnt via their super-task as well as in other ways. Then you can give each team a chance to identify three characteristics that make for a good season; these they can list on the Organising a Season of Games page. In addition each team could suggest things

Season Supertasks

► Seasons of sport come in all shapes and sizes. Using the Internet, compare four professional sports and represent the differences in a graph. For instance, you could represent the length of the season, the number of teams, or weeks of finals.

► Imagine your team finished at the bottom of the ladder after a season of sport. What are some of the things you could suggest to your team that they could do as a team to improve their position next season?

► Find a sport that interests you and research the way the season is constructed. Write a short report on anything you find interesting about the way the season is run.

► Interview a family member or friend who plays a sport. Prepare four questions to ask about the sport and the way the season works. What would you like to know?

► The word *season* has several meanings related and unrelated to sport. Record as many of those definitions as you can. Use your dictionary to help you.

► You have a group of 20 friends, including yourself, who together want to organise a season of downball (or some other game) at lunchtime. If you are going to play in pairs, figure out a way of organising the season so every pair gets to play every other pair at lunchtime across one week. Create a fixture so everyone knows when they will be playing.

► Research a sport (it might be the sport that you play or perhaps a friend plays), to find out how the season is organised so that the competition is fair.

► Write a creative story using the stem 'I only had to win one more game to get to the finals.'

► Make a list of all of the people required to make a season of sport successful. Start with the players.

► Investigate a sport and examine not only the written rules that make the game fair but the unwritten rules as well (for example, shaking hands after a game of tennis).

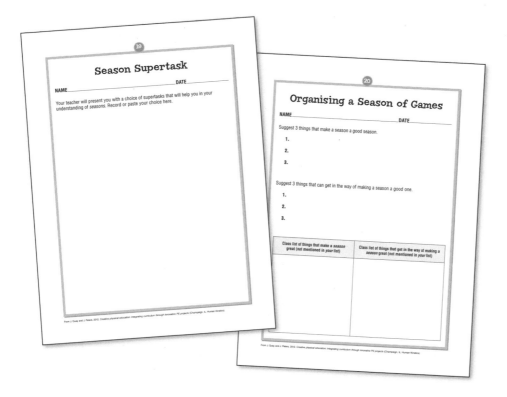

that get in the way of having a good season. Each team's suggestions can then be shared and class lists developed. These lists can be referred to when developing and agreeing on the structure of the season. While the round-robin structure is usually considered the most fair in this circumstance, the issue of finals can be contentious. Also of concern may be the points to be awarded during the season.

A ROUND ROBIN WITH FINALS

With our four teams, the fairest competition structure and the one that best helps us meet our teaching aims is probably some form of round-robin season. With four teams, this means at least three rounds with some finals (where the finals always involve all teams). Three rounds are really a minimum; over a school term it should be possible to play six season rounds with finals, or nine season rounds without finals. The more rounds, the more opportunities the students have for improvement when these are linked directly with practice sessions.

The round-robin season could be played without finals, as in the English Premier League soccer in which an overall winner is determined by the accruing of points from each season game. However, many young people would expect a season of games to have a finals series to determine the overall winning team. The other advantage of a finals series in which every team is involved is that the finals allow the season to start again. Even the team on the bottom of the ladder has a chance to redeem themselves. For many sporting codes, the finals series is a knockout competition. But this does not have to be the case in physical education.

Curriculum Integration

Visual Arts

Students employ art media, techniques and processes to develop a poster display that advertises the finals series, encouraging parents and other students to attend.

Mathematics (Number Operations)

The mathematics involved in continually constructing the ladder can be supported by work in fractions and percentages.

With four teams, a two-stage finals series (semi-finals and grand finals) should involve all four teams playing throughout. The playing arrangements for the semi-finals can be linked to performance during the preceding rounds, as recorded on the ladder. We have found that students appreciate a ladder system that awards points to every team for every game. For instance, a win may be worth 10 points on the ladder, a draw worth 9 points and a loss worth 8 points. You should earn some points for playing the game because it is participation aimed at eventual improvement that is most important. The points given to a win, draw and loss for a particular game send a message about the relative importance of each, even if they don't influence the proceedings mathematically.

The actual scores of the games can be used to calculate percentages that determine ladder positions. For one game, points scored by a team are divided by points scored against that team by the opposition. This provides a ratio or a fraction. These point tallies accumulate through the season; they are not just calculated for single games (except for round one of the season).

A key decision of the semi-finals is determining who should play whom. Should first on the ladder play the second place team, the third, or the fourth? These decisions can be opened up for discussion as part of the design of the season. If you want the competition more open, then first place could play third and second could play fourth. If you wanted to use the pairings to reward performance, then first place would play fourth and second play third.

It is then usual for the winner of each semi-finals game to play off for first and second. The two losing semi-finals teams should also play off for third and fourth. All teams should always be playing. While the students will be concerned about determining the winning team, the educational aim is to provide opportunities for meaningful involvement with the focus on improvement. The winning team should be congratulated, but this should be second in importance to the improvement everyone has made through the season and the creative PE project as a whole.

With this in mind, the class could create player and spectator codes of conduct, modeled perhaps on similar codes that exist for use by sporting clubs. These codes of conduct can build on student experiences thus far in the season in relation to incidents and issues that may have arisen. They can also help communicate to parents and other spectators the creative PE

Curriculum Integration

Language

Student involvement in the creation of these codes of conduct will necessitate development of procedural writing skills that communicate effectively with a diverse audience for this particular purpose.

Technology

As a team, students can employ a tool such as a wiki to collate all of their team details: pictures, logo and chant; their schedule of games or fixture; their interpretation of the rules; and whatever else is necessary as a source of team information.

emphasis on improvement, rather than just winning.

The culmination of the season is the finals day, with adequate preparation made for celebrating the improvements achieved across the whole creative PE project. A certificate should be provided that could be stuck into the workbook on the page allocated for this at the end. The Comments and Autographs page at the back can facilitate this culmination of not just the season, but the creative PE project as a whole.

Curriculum Integration

Geography

As students think beyond the end of the PE Project, they can investigate the local area (home or school) in relation to venues, (such as parks and sporting facilities) that provide opportunities for social physical activity. They can create community maps using technology tools that highlight these venues and the facilities provided.

CHAPTER 4

Practice

▶ **The All Rounders.**

The development of teams, a class game and a season structure all exist in order to provide a more meaningful context within which students will be moved to improve. Improvement is the aim of all facets of creative PE, and in order to improve, one needs to practise.

Engagement in practice draws on the urge to improve as a teammate and team through a season of games that one enjoys. Practice itself can mean many things. It can simply mean repeatedly playing the game. We have encountered students who, in their teams, decide to do this outside of physical education lessons, such as during recess and lunch times, when they are offered the opportunity to borrow the necessary equipment. Such an interest in their team and game reveals the level of engagement that can be achieved with creative PE.

But practice does not only mean playing lots of games. It can and should involve a more thoughtful approach that requires some form of analysis and then practice targeted at improvements in the necessary areas. There is much room here for the teacher to structure this analysis and facilitate the development of activities that support team practice in areas where it is needed. Supported by analysis, there are three main areas targeted for improvement via practice: game *tactics*, game *skills* and game *fitness*.

These three areas and their connection to practice can be investigated by students. The *practice* supertasks contribute to this investigation by asking students to inquire into the importance of practice as well as the nature of tactics, skills and fitness. Following are some ideas for practice supertasks. Students should be able to choose amongst these options for the supertask that they would most like to attempt and master, both in school and for homework.

Having completed the practice supertasks, students will be better placed to contribute to discussion around the importance of practice and the nature of tactics, skills and fitness. This discussion can initially occur in teams, with indi-

Practice Supertasks

▶ Write a short story about a time when you might not have practised as hard as you could. Start with the stem "If only I had done . . .'

▶ Think of a mini-game or drill that can help improve our fitness as we practise for our class game. Write the instructions using procedural text. Check that it is a good game by trying it to see if it makes you huff and puff.

▶ Choose a skill and decide *how* you should practise it in order to get better. Practise each day for two weeks and see if you do get better. Describe the skill, what you did to get better and how you know you got better.

▶ Fitness is an important part of practising for a game. Do some fitness activity with your family for half an hour. You might choose running, walking, swimming or something else you all enjoy. Find out what everyone thought about doing the activity and what might stop them from doing it again.

▶ Think about your favorite sport. What are three tactics involved in that sport that would help you and your team to play the game well? Explain.

▶ Write the following words into a table and beside them write a sport that you think requires these fitness components to be practised and developed: endurance, strength and flexibility.

▶ Create a word find using all the words you can think of that have to do with learning new skills, getting fit and practising. Make sure you list the words beneath the puzzle so someone else can search for those words.

▶ Cut a picture out of a newspaper of someone performing a skill. Research that skill using the Internet and write down *how* to perform the skill. In a three-minute demonstration, present this skill to your class and suggest two ideas for practising this skill so that you will get better at it.

▶ Interview your parents or another family member and ask them what skills you developed as a child through practice. How did you practise them to improve them? Crawling is one example. Think of three more.

▶ Write a short story about the time you won a game or a competition or scored for your team using a clever tactic. Maybe you dodged an opponent or intercepted a ball. Be sure to explain what the tactic was.

viduals contributing what they have learnt via their supertask as well as in other ways. You could then provide each team with an opportunity to identify three reasons why practice is important and three reasons why people don't practise. They can list these on The Importance of Practice sheet. Each team's suggestions can then be shared and class lists developed.

Further exploration of the notion of practice can then occur around student understanding of tactics, skills and fitness. These three areas are covered in the practice supertasks. Students can be referred to the Tactics, Skills and Fitness sheet to discuss these in their teams and to provide examples relevant to the class game that express their understanding. This then begins the process of students thinking about the tactics, skills and fitness activities that are important to the class game. As a class, they can discuss and agree on basic definitions of each term and then enter these into the workbook. These don't have to be perfect; it is more important that they guide the understanding of students, appropriate to their age.

With older students, the notion of tactics can evolve into specific strategies that the teams employ in order to improve their performances. Likewise, movement skills can focus on more than the techniques appropriate to fundamental or foundational skills and evolve to incorporate skills that emerge with the game, such as different types of passing. Older students can also more readily comprehend the connection between health-related fitness and fitness for the class game via exploration of issues of fitness, strength and flexibility, as well as nutrition.

Curriculum Integration

Health and Science

Students can investigate the increased nutritional requirements associated with physical activity. What does the body need when one is regularly involved in physical activity? What about an elite performer?

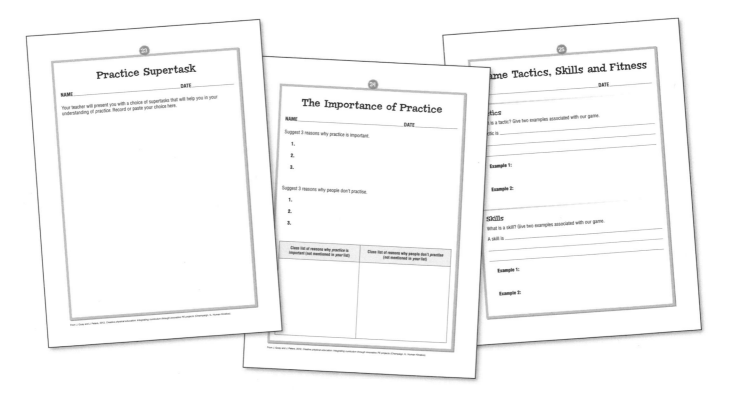

GAME TACTICS

Analysis of performance is most easily initiated with a discussion about how well the team are doing. Such a discussion should focus on each team as a whole, rather than on what an individual did right or wrong. From this whole team perspective, things that are being done well can be identified and documented. In addition there should be some thought put into what the team could do better, with suggestions for improvement (see the Game Tactics Review sheet).

These suggestions often take the form of tactics that the team can implement as they play the game. These tactics may be as simple as calling out to each other and as complex as developing set play strategies (see the Game Tactics Decision sheet). It is important that teams be able to develop these strategies and to practise them, either on their own or in practice games with other teams, allowing for timeouts for discussion. The teacher can play a pivotal role in asking questions targeting areas for improvement and making appropriate suggestions. These tactics can be shared around the class; however, they are often owned very privately by teams, who may think that sharing them would reduce their advantage in a game. It is successful development of these team tactics that is usually missing when teams only exist for short periods of time.

We are aware that some students may have little background in understanding tactics. If this is the case, you could introduce this notion via a simple game of tic-tac-toe (noughts and crosses) in pairs. Questions such as 'What did you do to win the game?' and 'How did you stop the other person winning?' may help to promote thinking and discussion of tactics.

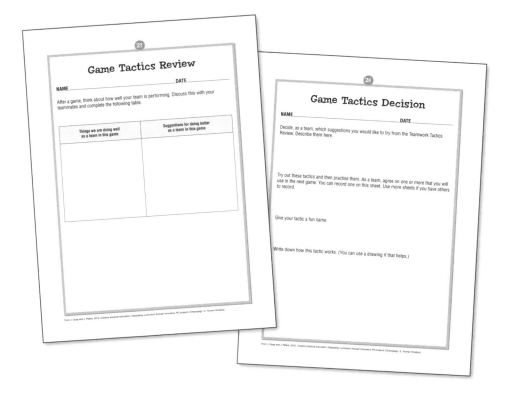

GAME SKILLS

Many traditional physical education lessons focus intently on movement or motor skill development because these are seen as the building blocks of improved performance. However, teachers of these lessons usually assume that the students can see the connections between these skills and the games they are playing; they also often assume that this connection is so obvious that the students will put effort into developing their skills in drills and other small group activities before they have even played a game. However, in these typical situations, there is little or no team affiliation, and there is no season; thus many students see this form of skill development as something they just have to do for the teacher in order to stay out of trouble.

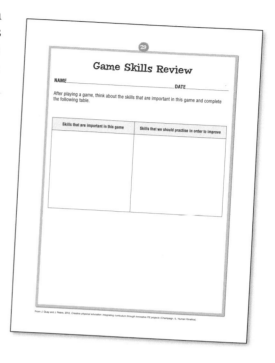

When team performance in the game is analyzed, a key area that is usually identified for improvement, apart from tactics, relates to skills. Students should be given the time to think about which skills are important to the game via the Game Skills Review. The skills that the teacher deemed must be included in the game when it was created should be amongst these. Other skills will, of course, also emerge as important in relation to the design of the class game.

GAME SKILL ANALYSIS AND FEEDBACK

When students realize that they, as a team, need to develop a particular game skill in order to improve their team's performance in a season of games, then they are usually much more motivated to engage in the effort required for practice. But improving performance of a game skill usually involves more than just doing it repetitively. It requires developing a better understanding of how the skill works (the techniques of the skill) and receiving feedback on how the student is actually performing the techniques.

The basic techniques or parts of a game skill are usually fairly obvious to students, and yet they are often conveyed to students as if they are teacher-derived facts to be learnt. This situates these techniques outside the everyday experience of young people. However, these techniques are familiar to many of them although many would not have stopped to observe and think about them.

Thus the first task in helping students to develop a game skill is to have them observe each other executing it in a controlled setting, such as throwing a ball to a partner to catch and return (or passing and receiving for older students). In this early analysis, the situation they observe will be fairly static: standing still. As their understanding progresses, these observations may be more accurately contextualized in mini-games and eventually in the season games. You will probably find that when the skill is contextualized in the game it changes subtly (or even significantly). This is why we have called them game skills rather than fundamental or foundational skills.

Mini-games allow for advanced analysis of game skills.

When students are observing each other, they should be watching the main parts of their teammate's body for what is going on:

Eyes—where are they looking or what are they looking at?

Arms and hands—what are their arms and hands doing?

Legs and feet—what are their legs and feet doing?

Torso—what is the main part of their body doing?

These observation activities can involve experimentation; they shouldn't simply be aimed at somehow determining the right answers. Trying different ways to perform the skill by doing different things with eyes, arms and hands, legs and feet, and torso, involves much more thought. Students will recognise amongst their teammates and classmates a range of techniques from which to choose. And for older students especially, it should become apparent that different techniques, even though part of the same skill, may be better used in different parts of the game. For example one type of throw may be important when scoring, another type when passing.

This analysis can be supported by the Game Skill Analysis sheet. Drawing stick figures to

Curriculum Integration

Visual Arts

Students apply visual arts techniques to animate their skill, for example by using modeling clay or producing a flip book to show the steps involved in the skill they have chosen. Still camera shots can also be used to assist in creating an animation.

portray the movement can be helpful. This is a task that could be supported by teams using their whiteboard and then sharing these drawings in class, for instance by the teacher taking photographs of the whiteboards and displaying them on a large screen. Multiple versions of this sheet can be used for the same game skill as students refine their understanding of this skill as it is used in the game.

Once the skill has been analyzed in a basic way, students in their teams can be asked to develop ways of practising this game skill. These activities may be drills or mini-games. The important thing is for the activity to involve repeated use of the skill in ways that are similar or identical to those of the class game. During these activities, students can be watching each other perform the skill. This may mean that for some of the activities there are teammates watching and describing other teammates' performance of this game skill so as to provide feedback using the Game Skill Feedback sheet.

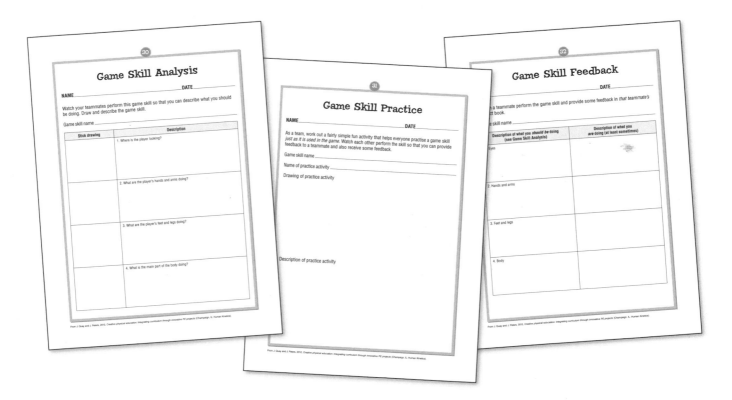

Curriculum Integration

Technology

Students can use a technology tool such as a digital camera, flip camera, video camera or something similar to record each other performing the game skills. Create a checklist of all the steps required in the skill and rate each other on each performance against those steps.

GAME FITNESS

Fitness is a very broad topic, as seen in the various interpretations of health-related fitness; these encompass cardiovascular endurance, muscular strength and endurance, flexibility and body composition. In creative PE, we are most concerned with game-related fitness, meaningful because it is associated with performance in the game although this can always have general health benefits. Game-related fitness usually concerns endurance, strength and flexibility. In terms

Push-ups can be part of a student-designed fitness circuit.

Curriculum Integration

Health and Science

Students can take their pulse at different times and investigate what that measurement may indicate in terms of health and the body's response to physical activity.

33

Fitness Circuit

NAME_____ DATE_____

Improving fitness can help improve your team's performance in the game. Work out a simple circuit, one that everyone in your team can do in 5 to 10 minutes, that improves fitness, strength and flexibility. Do these activities on a regular basis.

Fitness Activity

Name, draw and describe the activity for the circuit.

Number of times activity is to be completed

Strength Exercise

Name, draw and describe the strength exercise for the circuit.

Number of times exercise is to be completed

---

more easily understood by younger students, this translates into fitness activities, strength exercises and flexibility stretches.

The benefits from strength exercises and flexibility stretches will vary according to the age of the student. However, we believe that incorporating them into a fitness circuit will help introduce younger students to some of these activities, an advantage for them in later years at school and beyond.

A circuit is a relatively simple activity to manage. Students can develop their own activities for fitness, strength and flexibility. These can be as simple as running around the perimeter of the game space for fitness, doing sit-ups for strength and touching toes for flexibility. Other exercise and stretching ideas can be developed by each team, possibly as homework. Thus the fitness circuits can evolve under direction of each team.

When a fitness circuit is devised, the number of repetitions of each activity that each teammate will do should be decided upon. In this way individuals set their own goals for the activity; these can always be amended as improvement is achieved. Indeed the entire fitness circuit can be regularly changed by a team as new ideas for activities are developed. Taking one's pulse is another way of measuring improvement in fitness.

GAME STATISTICS

Once teams are familiar with how they can get involved in basic practice activities, they can think more deeply about the specific tactics, skills and areas of fitness that their team needs to practice. To help with this, more developed forms of analysis can be employed; these should involve some form of evidence collection. One way of collecting such evidence is to have players themselves, rather than observers, keep simple statistics, either during the game or by watching a video of the game.

In most games, a simple statistic can be connected with scoring. Which players scored? How many scores did they make? This statistic can have different meanings depending on the design of the game. Another simple statistic could focus on important skills in the game, for example, tracking successful catches and passes. The message gleaned from such statistics could be about improving the tactics, skills or fitness associated with the act of scoring.

Students are quite good at remembering, approximately at least, how many times they did significant things in a game. The short length of the class game (maybe five-minute halves for younger students) makes collecting these statistics at the end of a half or whole game easier. The Game Statistics page of the workbook enables a quick tally to be written down, even at half-time.

The statistics to be collected should be discussed by the teams and then as a class. The pros and cons of collecting particular statistics can then be debated, particularly in relation to the ease of counting and the relevance for improvement. Teams can, of course, collect different types of statistics. Younger students may only collect one statistic; older students may collect three or even more. These statistics can then be analyzed for a whole team, and even across teams. Graphs can be developed to better reveal how the team is doing if this is appropriate. Analysis of these statistics can be used to inform decisions regarding what needs to be practised. The teacher can also guide such decisions.

Curriculum Integration

Mathematics (Statistics and Probability)

Students can undertake statistical analysis using mean, median, mode and range to understand their performances as individuals and as a team.

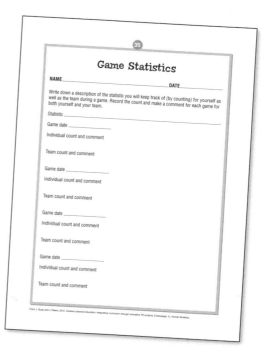

CELEBRATION

Towards the end of the season, preparation should be made for a celebratory culmination to the creative PE project. This could involve inviting parents or other community members to the final lesson. During this lesson all teams will be playing the finals games that involve playoffs for first, second, third and fourth (never last) positions. All teams are playing. The emphasis that day should be placed on the achievements of all teams and teammates across the various phases of their creative PE project: team, game, season and practice. This can be facilitated using the codes of conduct students prepared for players and spectators (see page 38).

One way to highlight these achievements is via certificates. These can be written like student reports as a personalized paragraph that describes important moments during

Curriculum Integration

Health and Science

Students can further practise health-enhancing behaviors by planning healthy snacks for an end-of-season celebration. Ensure they can justify their choice of snack.

their creative PE project when notable contributions were made. The certificate should celebrate achievements, especially those improvements achieved across the whole project in the areas of team, game, season and practice. These could be read at the celebration if appropriate. Students could stick their certificates on the allocated page in their workbooks.

Another way of celebrating the achievements of a creative PE project is to allow students to collect autographs; students may also contribute positive comments about teammates and others in other classmates' workbooks. A page has been allocated to this, but it may require two pages!

Shaking hands at the end of a game is a ritual that reminds students of the value of team play.

PART II

STUDENT WORKBOOK

Student Workbook

THIS BOOK BELONGS TO

_____

OUR TEAM

_____

OUR GAME

_____

By doing this creative PE project you will get a better understanding of being a great *team* member, making up great *games*, organising a fun *season*, and improving by *practising*.

My Team

NAME_____**DATE**_____

Stick a photo of your team here and label it with each teammate's name and nickname.

My team's name is _____

Make up a short song or chant connected with your team that you can use during the season to get everyone going. It must be friendly and positive.

My team's song or chant is

Team Profiles

NAME_____**DATE**_____

Collect information about each of your teammates. Add information as you get to know your teammates better.

Teammate's name	Teammate's strengths

From J. Quay and J. Peters, 2012, *Creative physical education: Integrating curriculum through innovative PE projects* (Champaign, IL: Human Kinetics).

Team Supertask

NAME_____**DATE**_____

Your teacher will present you with a choice of supertasks that will help you in your understanding of *teams*. Record or paste your choice here.

From J. Quay and J. Peters, 2012, *Creative physical education: Integrating curriculum through innovative PE projects* (Champaign, IL: Human Kinetics).

Being a Great Team

NAME_____**DATE**_____

Suggest 3 things that make a team great.

1.

2.

3.

Suggest 3 things that can get in the way of making a team great.

1.

2.

3.

Class list of things that make a *team* great (not mentioned in your list)	Class list of things that get in the way of making a *team* great (not mentioned in your list)

From J. Quay and J. Peters, 2012, *Creative physical education: Integrating curriculum through innovative PE projects* (Champaign, IL: Human Kinetics).

Recording Your Teammate Levels

NAME_____DATE_____

Level 4   I was respectful, I participated when asked, I was motivated and I was *caring* of others.

Level 3   I was respectful, I participated when asked and I was *motivated.*

Level 2   I was respectful and I *participated* when asked.

Level 1   I was *respectful.*

Level 0   I was *disrespectful.*

▶ **Lesson date** _____

Which level best describes you as a teammate in this lesson?

Write down one thing you did that shows you were at this level.

Were you ever disrespectful in this lesson?

▶ **Lesson date** _____

Which level best describes you in this lesson as a teammate?

Write down one thing you did that shows you were at this level.

Were you ever disrespectful in this lesson?

From J. Quay and J. Peters, 2012, *Creative physical education: Integrating curriculum through innovative PE projects* (Champaign, IL: Human Kinetics).

Teammate Levels Table

NAME_____**DATE**_____

Use this table to keep a record of how well you did in each class. Color in the square of the level which best described you in that class.

	Level 0—disrespectful	Level 1—respectful	Level 2—participated	Level 3—motivated	Level 4—caring
Lesson date					
Lesson date					
Lesson date					
Lesson date					
Lesson date					
Lesson date					
Lesson date					
Lesson date					

From J. Quay and J. Peters, 2012, *Creative physical education: Integrating curriculum through innovative PE projects* (Champaign, IL: Human Kinetics).

Teammate Levels
Role Play

NAME_____**DATE**_____

Use this as a work page to make up a role play with your teammates. Each teammate has to decide which level to role play in the scene you will act out. All the levels should be represented (including 0).

Describe very briefly what the role play is about.

List each of your teammates, the level that each will show in the role play and what each teammate will be doing.

Student's name	Teammate level and what each will be doing

From J. Quay and J. Peters, 2012, *Creative physical education: Integrating curriculum through innovative PE projects* (Champaign, IL: Human Kinetics).

Teammate Levels Discussions

NAME_____**DATE**_____

List each of the people on the team performing the role play and write down the level you think each is showing and why. Discuss this with your team.

Student's name	Teammate level and why you think this

List each of the people on the team performing the role play and write down the level you think each is showing and why. Discuss this with your team.

Student's name	Teammate level and why you think this

Game Supertask

NAME_____**DATE**_____

Your teacher will present you with a choice of supertasks that will help you in your understanding of *games*. Record or paste your choice here.

From J. Quay and J. Peters, 2012, *Creative physical education: Integrating curriculum through innovative PE projects* (Champaign, IL: Human Kinetics).

Making a Great Game

NAME_____ DATE_____

Suggest 3 things that make a game really great.

1.

2.

3.

Suggest 3 things that can get in the way of making a game really great.

1.

2.

3.

Class list of things that make a *game* great (not mentioned in your list)	Class list of things that get in the way of making a *game* great (not mentioned in your list)

From J. Quay and J. Peters, 2012, *Creative physical education: Integrating curriculum through innovative PE projects* (Champaign, IL: Human Kinetics).

Cooking Up Your Game

NAME_____**DATE**_____

When you cook up your game, you must think about these ingredients:

Enjoyment—Obviously, your game should be fun for everyone in your class to play!

Participation—*All* players must be playing in the game *all* the time. The game must be easy enough that everyone in the class can play the game.

Safety—The game must not involve any situations in which there is a fair chance that players could be hurt.

Skills—The teacher will give you a skill or skills that your game must include. The more often these are used in your game the better the game.

Equipment—Each team has the same equipment. You don't need to use all of it in your game. When you play another team in a game, you will be able to use their equipment as well as your own.

Time—The game should have two halves of an agreed amount of time.

Space—Games between teams will take up half of the total space. When not playing an actual game, your team will have a quarter of the space to plan and practise in.

Umpire or referee—Your game must be simple enough that it can be played *without* an umpire or referee.

Scoring—There must be some system of scoring, and it must be simple enough that scoring can be done by the players. There will be no special scorer.

From J. Quay and J. Peters, 2012, *Creative physical education: Integrating curriculum through innovative PE projects* (Champaign, IL: Human Kinetics).

Game Review

NAME_____**DATE**_____

Give your book to someone on the other team who will write the review of your game.

Name of team whose game is being reviewed _____

Name of team doing review _____

Enjoyment

What parts of this game were the most fun?

Give a mark out of 10 for how much fun the game was.

1	2	3	4	5	6	7	8	9	10

Not much fun   Extremely fun

Participation

How easy was it for everyone on both teams to *join in* and *play* this game?

Give a mark out of 10 for the amount of playing you got to do in this game.

1	2	3	4	5	6	7	8	9	10

Very little   Whole game

Safety

How *safe* was this game? Write down any unsafe situations that occurred during the game.

Give a mark out of 10 for how safe the game was.

1	2	3	4	5	6	7	8	9	10

Not very safe   Extremely safe

Skills

How much did the game involve the *skills* the teacher set for you to include?

Give a mark out of 10 for how much you had to use these skills in the game.

1	2	3	4	5	6	7	8	9	10

Never   Always

Equipment

How clever was the *way* the equipment was used in this game? This is not about making the game complicated but making it great to play.

Give a mark out of 10 for how cleverly this game used the equipment.

1	2	3	4	5	6	7	8	9	10

Not very cleverly   Extremely cleverly

Umpire or Referee and Scoring

How easy was it to follow the rules and score this game?

Give a mark out of 10 for how easy the game was to understand and score.

1	2	3	4	5	6	7	8	9	10

Not very easy   Extremely easy

Other Comments

Think about your answers to these questions. What suggestions can you now make to improve this game?

Our Class Game

NAME_____**DATE**_____

Describe the overall *aim* of the game (how a team scores).

Draw or paste a *diagram* of this class game here. (Include the boundaries, the placing of equipment and the positions of players.)

List different player positions and what they *can* do.

List different player positions and what they *can't* do.

Game Review of Class Game

NAME_____**DATE**_____

Name of class game _____

Enjoyment

What parts of this game were the most *fun*?

Give a mark out of 10 for how much fun the game was.

1	2	3	4	5	6	7	8	9	10

Not much fun   Extremely fun

Participation

How easy was it for everyone on both teams to *join in* and *play* this game?

Give a mark out of 10 for the amount of playing you got to do in this game.

1	2	3	4	5	6	7	8	9	10

Not very easy   Extremely easy

Safety

How *safe* was this game? Write down any unsafe situations that occurred during the game.

Give a mark out of 10 for how safe the game was.

1	2	3	4	5	6	7	8	9	10

Not very safe   Extremely safe

(continued)

Skills

How much did the game involve the *skills* the teacher set to include?

Give a mark out of 10 for how much you had to use these skills in the game.

| 1 | 2 | 3 | 4 | 5 | 6 | 7 | 8 | 9 | 10 |

Never   Always

Equipment

How cleverly was the equipment used in this game? This is not about making the game complicated but making it great to play.

Give a mark out of 10 for how cleverly this game used the equipment.

| 1 | 2 | 3 | 4 | 5 | 6 | 7 | 8 | 9 | 10 |

Not very cleverly   Extremely cleverly

Umpire or Referee and Scoring

How easy was it to follow the rules and score this game?

Give a mark out of 10 for how easy the game was to understand and score.

| 1 | 2 | 3 | 4 | 5 | 6 | 7 | 8 | 9 | 10 |

Not very easy   Extremely easy

Other Comments

Think about your answers. What suggestions can you now make to improve this game?

From J. Quay and J. Peters, 2012, *Creative physical education: Integrating curriculum through innovative PE projects* (Champaign, IL: Human Kinetics).

Our Class Game—Final

NAME_____**DATE**_____

The *name* of this game _____

Describe the overall *aim* of this game (how a team scores).

Draw or paste a *diagram* of this class game here. (Include the boundaries, the placing of equipment and the positions of players.)

List the different player positions and what they *can* do.

List the different player positions and what they *can't* do.

Season Supertask

NAME_____**DATE**_____

Your teacher will present you with a choice of supertasks that will help you in your understanding of *seasons*. Record or paste your choice here.

From J. Quay and J. Peters, 2012, *Creative physical education: Integrating curriculum through innovative PE projects* (Champaign, IL: Human Kinetics).

Organising a Season of Games

NAME_____**DATE**_____

Suggest 3 things that make a season a good season.

1.

2.

3.

Suggest 3 things that can get in the way of making a season a good one.

1.

2.

3.

Class list of things that make a *season* great (not mentioned in *your* list)	Class list of things that get in the way of making a *season* great (not mentioned in *your* list)

Season

NAME _____

DATE _____

ROUND 1	ROUND 2	ROUND 3	SEMI-FINALS	FINALS
versus	versus		(1st on ladder) versus (4th on ladder)	(semi-finals 1st) versus (semi-finals 2nd)
versus	versus	versus	(2nd on ladder) versus (3rd on ladder)	(semi-finals 3rd) versus (semi-finals 4th)

21

Season Ladder

NAME _____ DATE _____

Teams (alphabetical order)	ROUND 1			ROUND 2			ROUND 3		
	Score	Points	Position	Score	Points	Position	Score	Points	Position

Win = 10 points, draw = 9 points, loss = 8 points

From J. Quay and J. Peters, 2012, *Creative physical education: Integrating curriculum through innovative PE projects* (Champaign, IL: Human Kinetics).

Practice Supertask

NAME_____**DATE**_____

Your teacher will present you with a choice of supertasks that will help you in your understanding of *practice*. Record or paste your choice here.

From J. Quay and J. Peters, 2012, *Creative physical education: Integrating curriculum through innovative PE projects* (Champaign, IL: Human Kinetics).

The Importance of Practice

NAME_____DATE_____

Suggest 3 reasons why practice is important.

    1.

    2.

    3.

Suggest 3 reasons why people don't practise.

    1.

    2.

    3.

Class list of reasons why *practice* is important (not mentioned in *your* list)	Class list of reasons why people don't *practise* (not mentioned in *your* list)

From J. Quay and J. Peters, 2012, *Creative physical education: Integrating curriculum through innovative PE projects* (Champaign, IL: Human Kinetics).

Game Tactics, Skills and Fitness

NAME_____DATE_____

Tactics

What is a tactic? Give two examples associated with our game.

A tactic is _____

_____

_____

Example 1:

Example 2:

Skills

What is a skill? Give two examples associated with our game.

A skill is _____

_____

_____

Example 1:

Example 2:

Fitness

What is fitness? Give two examples of ways you can keep fit for our game.

Fitness is _____

_____

_____

Example 1:

Example 2:

From J. Quay and J. Peters, 2012, *Creative physical education: Integrating curriculum through innovative PE projects* (Champaign, IL: Human Kinetics).

Game Tactics Review

NAME_____DATE_____

After a game, think about how well your team is performing. Discuss this with your teammates and complete the following table.

Things we are doing well as a team in this game	Suggestions for doing better as a team in this game

From J. Quay and J. Peters, 2012, *Creative physical education: Integrating curriculum through innovative PE projects* (Champaign, IL: Human Kinetics).

Game Tactics Decision

NAME_____**DATE**_____

Decide, as a team, which suggestions you would like to try from the Teamwork Tactics Review. Describe them here.

Try out these tactics and then practise them. As a team, agree on one or more that you will use in the next game. You can record one on this sheet. Use more sheets if you have others to record.

Give your tactic a fun name.

Write down how this tactic works. (You can use a drawing if that helps.)

Game Skills Review

NAME_____DATE_____

After playing a game, think about the skills that are important in this game and complete the following table.

Skills that are important in this game	Skills that we should practise in order to improve

From J. Quay and J. Peters, 2012, *Creative physical education: Integrating curriculum through innovative PE projects* (Champaign, IL: Human Kinetics).

Game Skill Analysis

NAME_____**DATE**_____

Watch your teammates perform this game skill so that you can describe what you should be doing. Draw and describe the game skill.

Game skill name _____

Stick drawing	Description
	1. Where is the player looking?
	2. What are the player's hands and arms doing?
	3. What are the player's feet and legs doing?
	4. What is the main part of the body doing?

From J. Quay and J. Peters, 2012, *Creative physical education: Integrating curriculum through innovative PE projects* (Champaign, IL: Human Kinetics).

Game Skill Practice

NAME_____**DATE**_____

As a team, work out a fairly simple fun activity that helps everyone practise a game skill *just as it is used in the game.* Watch each other perform the skill so that you can provide feedback to a teammate and also receive some feedback.

Game skill name _____

Name of practice activity _____

Drawing of practice activity

Description of practice activity

From J. Quay and J. Peters, 2012, *Creative physical education: Integrating curriculum through innovative PE projects* (Champaign, IL: Human Kinetics).

Game Skill Feedback

NAME_____**DATE**_____

Watch a teammate perform the game skill and provide some feedback in *that teammate's* project book.

Game skill name _____

Description of what you *should be* doing (see Game Skill Analysis)	Description of what you *are* doing (at least sometimes)
1. Eyes	
2. Hands and arms	
3. Feet and legs	
4. Body	

From J. Quay and J. Peters, 2012, *Creative physical education: Integrating curriculum through innovative PE projects* (Champaign, IL: Human Kinetics).

Fitness Circuit

NAME_____ **DATE**_____

Improving fitness can help improve your team's performance in the game. Work out a simple *circuit*, one that *everyone* in your team can do in 5 to 10 minutes, that improves fitness, strength and flexibility. Do these activities on a regular basis.

Fitness Activity

Name, draw and describe the activity for the circuit.

Number of times activity is to be completed

Strength Exercise

Name, draw and describe the strength exercise for the circuit.

Number of times exercise is to be completed

Flexibility Stretch

Name, draw and describe the stretch for the circuit.

Number of times stretch is to be completed

Tick a box each time you complete the entire fitness circuit.

1	2	3	4	5

From J. Quay and J. Peters, 2012, *Creative physical education: Integrating curriculum through innovative PE projects* (Champaign, IL: Human Kinetics).

Game Statistics

NAME_____**DATE**_____

Write down a description of the statistic you will keep track of (by counting) for yourself as well as the team during a game. Record the count and make a comment for each game for both yourself and your team.

Statistic _____

Game date _____

Individual count and comment

Team count and comment

Game date _____

Individual count and comment

Team count and comment

Game date _____

Individual count and comment

Team count and comment

Game date _____

Individual count and comment

Team count and comment

From J. Quay and J. Peters, 2012, *Creative physical education: Integrating curriculum through innovative PE projects* (Champaign, IL: Human Kinetics).

PE Project Certificate

NAME_____**DATE**_____

(Stick your certificate here.)

From J. Quay and J. Peters, 2012, *Creative physical education: Integrating curriculum through innovative PE projects* (Champaign, IL: Human Kinetics).

Celebration

NAME_____**DATE**_____

Now that you have successfully completed your creative PE project, use this page to collect positive comments and autographs from people in your team, in other teams and from anyone else (for example, your family) who has helped you during this project.

As we stated at the beginning, creative PE is a class project. But this project does not focus on a topic. Rather, as you can now see, this project emphasizes student engagement by tapping into their interests, but not just in a shallow way. It grabs them by opening a space to explore the question 'Who am I?' which is always at one with the question 'Who are we?'

Creative PE asks young people to be great teammates, clever game creators and designers, fair-minded season architects and analytical practice trainers. All of these together give us the young person who has the skills and understanding to work with others in arranging meaningful opportunities for participation in social physical activity. No longer are they just students. No longer are they dependent on adults to organise sports for them. No longer are they just players. They are now much, much more.

As you have seen, we have incorporated signposts for possible curriculum integration throughout the text. These are just the beginning. There are many ways to adapt a creative PE project as an integrated unit. To help you build these curricular relationships, we include an appendix that overviews the connections between creative PE and curricula in various countries.

It is always our expectation that you, the teacher, will customize a creative PE project for your class. The templates are all designed to be manipulated so that you can meet your planning needs. So we would love to hear from you at jquay@unimelb.edu.au and jacqui.peters@deakin.edu.au if you have further ideas or questions. None of us ever stops learning. And we can always be better teachers.

We wish you all the very best in your teaching!

John Quay and Jacqui Peters

Creative PE and International Physical Education Standards

Creative PE has been designed to support contemporary school curricula in a range of nations including Australia, New Zealand, the USA and the UK. We believe that similarities among physical education curricula in these places can be seen when characterised across six broad themes that also typify a creative PE project.

- Students participate in regular moderate to vigorous physical activity.
- Students develop competent movement skills and techniques associated with games.
- Students value physical activity for health, social interaction and challenge.
- Students understand movement principles, strategies, concepts and means for improvement (analysis).
- Students develop personal and social responsibility: rules, conventions, fair play and safe participation.
- Students understand the contribution of physical activity to health, well-being and the community.

These themes reflect the breadth of application of creative PE when considered against various physical education curricula. However, we believe that creative PE offers the most benefits when curriculum integration is the goal. Such integration is best achieved when teachers retain responsibility for *how* the curriculum standards that guide their work are interpreted in practice.

National curriculum standards for physical education in the United States describe students who are competent movers participating in regular physical activity in order to maintain fitness, who understand principles and strategies of games, who demonstrate respectful behaviors and value activity for a range of reasons including social interaction. These standards are available for interpretation at state and district levels. They are readily achieved through a creative PE project.

New national curriculum standards for physical education are being developed in the UK for implementation in 2013. These will be less prescriptive than the current standards, allowing greater flexibility for teachers. The current standards most relevant to creative PE require teachers to teach the following: motor and movement skills, tactics and game principles as well as how to improve in all of these areas; safe participation, working within rules, cooperation and teamwork; and the relationship of fitness and physical activity to health.

The national curriculum standards in Australia are similarly in flux; a new Australian curriculum addressing health and physical education is due for implementation in 2013. Until the national curriculum is implemented, the standards have mainly been those developed by states and territories. Currently, the physical education standards of the various states and territories of Australia encourage learning a range of physical, thinking and social skills similar to those encouraged through creative PE. It is expected that more general capabilities will be integrated with physical education in the new curriculum standards, including literacy, numeracy, critical and creative thinking, ethical behaviour and personal and social competence, further exemplifying connections with creative PE.

The New Zealand health and physical education curriculum is also highly integrated: it incorporates movement, bodies, attitudes, values, social skills, critical thinking and decision making, all in relation to both the individual and the community. Here physical education is highly integrated with health and well-being. Such integration is well supported by creative PE.

Curricular Themes Characterizing the Physically Educated Student

	USA	UK	Australia	New Zealand
Is a competent mover—skills, techniques, games	✓	✓	✓	✓
Understands movement principles, strategies, concepts and means for improvement (analysis)	✓	✓	✓	✓
Participates in regular moderate to vigorous physical activity, maintaining and improving fitness	✓	✓	✓	✓
Values physical activity for health, social interaction and challenge	✓	✓	✓	✓
Develops personal and social responsibility: rules, conventions, fair play and safe participation	✓	✓	✓	✓
Understands the contribution of physical activity to health, well-being and the community	✓	✓	✓	✓

In summary, two important principles stand out.

- The important themes that arise from each curriculum are achievable through a creative PE project.
- Teachers have some scope to determine *how* curriculum standards are to be achieved in practice, enabling them to work creatively to integrate the curriculum via programs such as creative PE.

RECOMMENDED READINGS

This is a list of readings that will further support your understanding of creative PE. It is by no means exhaustive.

Almond, L. (1983). Games making. *Bulletin of Physical Education, 19*(1), 32-35.

Butler, J.I., & Griffin, L.L. (2010). *More teaching games for understanding: Moving globally.* Champaign, IL: Human Kinetics.

Curtner-Smith, M.D. (1996). Teaching games for understanding: Using games invention with elementary children. *Journal of Physical Education, Recreation & Dance,* 67(3), 33-37.

Griffin, L.L., & Butler, J.I. (2005). *Teaching games for understanding.* Champaign, IL: Human Kinetics.

Hastie, P. (2010). *Student-designed games: Strategies for promoting creativity, cooperation, and skill development.* Champaign, IL: Human Kinetics.

Hellison, D. (2010). *Teaching personal and social responsibility through physical activity* (3rd ed.). Champaign, IL: Human Kinetics.

Launder, A.G., & Piltz, W. (2001). *Play practice.* Champaign, IL: Human Kinetics.

Quay, J. & Peters, J. (2008). Skills, strategies, sport and social responsibility: Reconnecting physical education. *Journal of Curriculum Studies, 40*(5), 601-626.

Siedentop, D. (1994). *Sport education: Quality PE through positive sport experiences.* Champaign, IL: Human Kinetics.

Werner, P., Thorpe, R., & Bunker, D. (1996). Teaching games for understanding: Evolution of a model. *Journal of Physical Education, Recreation & Dance, 67*(1), 28-33.

Here we are! Jacqui Peters on the left, Meg Alexander from Roberts McCubbin Primary School in the middle, and John Quay on the right. The photographs in this book are all of Meg's grade three/four class.

John Quay, PhD, is a lecturer in the graduate school of education at the University of Melbourne (Melbourne, Victoria, Australia), where he works with preservice teachers in primary and secondary teacher education.

Quay has many years of experience working in outdoor education and as a teacher and coordinator of physical education and sport at the middle school and junior high levels. As a researcher, he has published more than 15 scholarly articles on physical education, experiential education, outdoor and environmental education, and educational philosophy.

Quay is a member of the Australian Council for Health, Physical Education and Recreation (ACHPER) and has served as a member of the ACHPER Victorian Board. He is also a member of the Australian College of Education (MACE), Australian Council for Educational Leaders (MACEL), the Philosophy of Education Society of Australia (PESA), and the Victorian Outdoor Education Association (VOEA).

In 1999, Quay received the Victorian Inspirational Environmental Education Teacher Award from Ford One Planet Environment Awards In his free time, Quay enjoys bushwalking, skiing, running, and cycling.

Jacqui Peters, ME, is a lecturer in the department of health and physical education at Deakin University in Burwood, Victoria, Australia, where she has worked primarily with preservice elementary classroom teachers since 2002.

Peters taught K-12 physical education for 15 years before teaching at the university level. Her work as a practitioner and her current research keep her in contact with the state of physical education in the schools and, in particular, issues facing classroom teachers responsible for physical education instruction.

Peters has published three journal articles pertaining to *Creative Physical Education* and has presented the project at numerous conferences. Peters is also a frequent presenter of practical and theoretical sessions at Australian Council for Health, Physical Education, and Recreation (ACHPER) state conferences and in schools as a consultant for health and physical education. She is a member of ACHPER and also a member and the convener of the Health and Physical Education Tertiary Alliance-Victoria (HPETA-V). An active supporter of community sport, Peters volunteers as both a youth coach and committee member.

Currently a PhD candidate in physical education at Deakin University, Peters holds a graduate diploma in business (sport management) in addition to a master's degree in education. Peters and her family live in Box Hill South, Victoria, Australia. In her free time she enjoys walking, practicing yoga, and reading.

You'll find other outstanding
physical education resources at
www.HumanKinetics.com

HOW TO USE THIS CD-ROM

SYSTEM REQUIREMENTS

You can use this CD-ROM on either a Windows-based PC or a Macintosh computer.

Windows

- IBM PC compatible with Pentium processor
- Windows 2000/XP/Vista/7
- Adobe Reader 8.0
- Microsoft Office PowerPoint 2003 or higher
- 4x CD-ROM drive

Macintosh

- Power Mac recommended
- System 10.4 or higher
- Adobe Reader
- Microsoft Office PowerPoint 2004 for MAC or higher
- 4x CD-ROM drive

USER INSTRUCTIONS

Windows

1. Insert the *Creative Physical Education: Integrating Curriculum Through Innovative PE Projects* CD-ROM. (Note: The CD-ROM must be present in the drive at all times.)
2. Select the "My Computer" icon from the desktop.
3. Select the CD-ROM drive.
4. Open the file you wish to view. See the "CD Contents.pdf" file in the "00_Read Me First" folder for a list of the contents.

Macintosh

1. Insert the *Creative Physical Education: Integrating Curriculum Through Innovative PE Projects* CD-ROM. (Note: The CD-ROM must be present in the drive at all times.)
2. Double-click the CD icon located on the desktop.
3. Open the file you wish to view. See the "CD Contents.pdf" file in the "00 Read Me First" folder for a list of the contents.

For customer support, contact Technical Support:

Phone: 217-351-5076 Monday through Friday (excluding holidays) between 7:00 a.m. and 7:00 p.m. (CST).

Fax: 217-351-2674

E-mail: support@hkusa.com